Lenna Bicke

November 26, 1915 - Novem

Lenna with sunflowers – in France, 1999

*L*enna Bickerton died on November 14, 1999, shortly before her 84th birthday. She had lived most of her life in Rudheath, the setting for her two books, "Memories of a Cheshire Childhood" and "We'll Gather Lilacs...".

Through the years the area changed from a quiet rural hamlet to a busy suburb of Northwich. Lenna chronicled the changes, accurately observed and remembered.

Lenna spent her working life in the family grocery and greengrocery business, first with her parents, Edith and James Cloudsdale, and then with her husband, Jim.

After their retirement, Lenna was at last to develop her talents – writing and painting. All her life she had loved literature, art and music.

At the age of 69 she began painting in oils – charming landscapes and flower subjects. Her book, first published in 1996, is now in its eighth impression. It was the first book to be produced by the Léonie Press and has been enjoyed by readers locally and all over the world. One academic compared Lenna's writing to that of Mrs Gaskell.

Lenna was married to James (Jim) Bickerton for 59 years until his death in 1996. Their two daughters are Vivien Wilson, formerly of Rudheath and now of Winsford, and June Hall, who lives in the Yorkshire Dales. Vivien and her husband Peter have a daughter, Lorna, and two sons, Jamie and Stuart.

Lenna often wished that she had been able to travel but that opportunity only came in her last years. In 1999 she spent holidays in France and Norway, where her grandson Stuart and his son Jostein then lived.

She is missed by her family, and many friends and neighbours, but has left a lasting achievement for all to enjoy.

Her funeral was held at Rudheath Parish Church. A copy of her first book and one of her paintings were placed near the coffin during the service. Lenna was buried at Rudheath Cemetery, where her beloved Jim also lies.

January 2008

LENNA BICKERTON

MEMORIES OF A CHESHIRE CHILDHOOD

Léonie Press

Dedicated with love to my Mother
Florence Lenna Bickerton, 1996

Original ISBNs
1 901253 00 7 and 1 901253 13 9
ISBN13 for memorial edition
978-1-901253-13-9

First published September 1996
Reprinted November 1996
Reprinted April 1997
Reprinted February 1998
Memorial edition published February 2000
Memorial edition reprinted December 2002
Memorial edition reprinted December 2004
Memorial edition reprinted January 2008

© Lenna Bickerton

All rights reserved. No part of this publication may be reproduced, stored in a retrieval system, or transmitted in any form or by any means, electronic, mechanical, photocopying, recording or otherwise, without the prior permission of the copyright owner.

Edited, typeset and published in Gt Britain by:
Léonie Press
an imprint of
Anne Loader Publications
13 Vale Road, Hartford
Northwich, Cheshire CW8 1PL
e-mail: anne@leoniepress.com
Website: www.leoniepress.com

Printed by:
Poplar Services, St Helens, Merseyside
Covers laminated by: The Finishing Touch, St Helens

Contents

Chapter One ...p1
Introducing Mother and my Grandparents

Chapter Two... p7
A heroic rescue; Granny; the neighbours

Chapter Three ... p17
Grandad; infant schooldays; home industry

Chapter Four ... p22
May Days; a new Dad; back to Granny's

Chapter Five ... p31
An ideal home; Rudheath School

Chapter Six ... p39
Rambles; the canal; local people

Chapter Seven ... p48
Pits and flashes; Children's games; boat horses

Chapter Eight ... p55
Sunday School treat; life at home; dancing troupe

Chapter Nine ... p62
Home remedies; Rosie; New Brighton

Chapter Ten ... p71
Adventures; cinemas; old Northwich

The author would like to
thank all the kind people
whose help and advice have
contributed to the writing
and publication of this book.

Chapter One

Mother aged about 18

There were many like my mother, a young war widow, who took the places of young men called up to fight for their country. One of my earliest memories is being taken to see her at work unloading a cargo of bricks from a narrow-boat.

*D*uring the first World War, I lived with my grandparents. My mother, a young war widow, went out to work at the firm of Brunner Mond & Co. There were many like her, who took the places of young men called up to fight for their country, and one of my earliest recollections of this period is of being taken to see her at work. She was helping to unload a cargo of bricks from a narrow-boat pulled up alongside the jetty, the chemical factory being built beside the Trent and Mersey Canal at Lostock. Some of her workmates made a fuss of me as I stood there with my young aunt on the canal bank. They were clad in khaki overalls similar to a boilersuit and wore a kind of mob-cap pulled well over their ears, completely enveloping their hair.

Times were difficult but there were lighter moments. One night, she was working with another young woman at the top of a high building nicknamed "The Towers". She had stepped out onto the landing for a breath of fresh air. It was a very dark night and away in the distance she spotted a light which kept going in and out. She called her friend to see what she could make of it, and, after an earnest discussion, they decided that it was someone signalling.

Only a few nights previously, the manager had asked them to report anything which appeared untoward or suspicious. They were "dangerous times and one never knew where the enemy might be lurking", he had said. The young women decided to report what they had seen and the chargehand told the foreman, who sent out two men to investigate. They returned after a while, mission accomplished. It turned out to be the night-soil men emptying the earth closets, way out in the fields. As they progressed, the light from the storm lamp hanging on the back of the cart kept disappearing and re-appearing as it swung to and fro! Seen from a very high building, it did look as though signals were being sent out to some person or persons unknown. Poor Mother — it was very embarrassing to her, and yet she was only carrying out orders: being zealous as instructed. In the event, she was commended by the manager for having been alert!

The war dragged on, for longer than everyone had expected, and Mother was directed to a newly built Government factory at Wincham, where ammunition was made. It, too, was close to the canal, for easy access. What a boon those Inland Waterways were during that terrible war.

Many young girls, and indeed older women, came in from outlying villages and towns to work here. Some of them spoke in a very broad Cheshire dialect, almost non-existent now. Young folk of today would be hard pressed to understand what was being said. They worked very hard, and roughed it quite a lot, but in spite of the hardships, were seldom downhearted. More often than not, they sang to keep up their spirits, and enjoyed being together. Eventually, I learned the songs off by heart — melodies such as "Keep the home fires burning", "Tipperary", "Take me back to dear old Blighty", "Pack up your troubles" and many more.

Mother and her workmates were involved in making some kind of crystals. Large centrifuges (which the girls called "fugals") were filled with a chemical liquid and then these machines revolved rapidly until it turned into fine crystals. These were then poured down a chute into trucks which stood below. When these were filled, the crystals were transferred into sacks and placed in the waiting narrow-boats on the canal.

Mother and her colleagues on shift-work were paid around three pounds, five shillings a week, which seemed like a small fortune to them. Even so, they all longed for the war to end. Little did they realise what hard times were in store for the young men returning home. My grandparents had two sons serving with the Forces in France, and another working in the Belfast shipyards, so this was a very anxious time for them too.

A malignant type of influenza was rife in the country at this time — I believe it was known as "Spanish 'flu" — and some people in the town died from its effects. Various members of our family went down with it, including my mother, though I never caught it.

The war came to an end, and, as my mother was working on the night-shift, on 11th November 1918, she asked Granny to waken her in time to hear the works' buzzer blow, signalling that the Armistice had been signed, and joined the large crowd at the top of the street.

After the war was over, there was very little work for women, apart from going into domestic service, and this is what Mother did, leaving me in Granny's care. She came home on her days off, travelling from Manchester on the "dripping train", as it was nicknamed by the local lads. This was because the girls often carried home with them a pot of dripping, on Sunday afternoons, given to them by their mistresses — usually a tasty bit left over from the roast beef! A lot of hard work, and not a great deal of remuneration: that was the order of the day.

I look back with great affection to the years that I spent with my grandparents. On winter mornings, Grandad would be the first to rise, and by the time that Granny and I had come downstairs, a coal fire would be blazing in the black-leaded grate. How cosy it was, eating our breakfast together. It was always the same — duck-eggs. They looked enormous to me in their bluey-green shells; a whole one for Grandad and a half each for Granny and me. When mornings were dark, the paraffin lamp high on the mantelshelf cast its golden glow around us and I felt full of happiness.

Grandad was a boilermaker by trade, and wore moleskin trousers for work. They looked like smooth grey velvet. In his younger days he had been a journeyman, working at either of the boat-builders in the town, Pimblotts or Yarwoods. His employers knew him as a very good workman.

Alas, in this younger period of his life, there had been a darker side to his character. He did what lots of his fellow-workers did, and went drinking at the many public houses in the town, which stayed open all hours. The owners often encouraged the men to bring along their own food, so that some never went home until late at night. It also encouraged them to neglect their families and waste their money, if they were foolish enough to do so. I have heard Granny say that Grandad was paid in gold sovereigns: how few or how many I don't know, but she should be lucky to receive one for keeping house. That was, of course, until he "learned some sense".

I have also heard her say more than once, "Sam, you should have owned a row of houses for the money that's passed through your hands!"

It's amazing how far a sovereign would stretch in those days. People of that era have told me that a fresh loaf cost twopence halfpenny (old money), and twopence when a day old. Similarly, cakes a day old were six for a penny. Two pounds of sugar cost twopence halfpenny, bacon was sixpence per pound, and you could buy a pennyworth of sugar and treacle straight from the barrel. Nancollis's, the grocers in Station Road, also ran a commercial hotel next door, cooking beef and ham for travellers. Children would be sent here to buy beef dripping with the lovely brown jelly and sediments still adhering to it for a penny or twopence, to be put on bread for their tea, and sometimes there would be a ham bone, with quite a lot of ham still left upon it, for the sum of threepence!

It must have been a constant source of anxiety to see Grandad dissipating his hard earned money away on a Saturday night. He often took on foolish wagers, egged on by his pals. One such stipulated that he should run from the Old Cock Hotel in Northwich to Knutsford jail, seven miles away, in his stockinged feet, and back again. This he did in good time and won his wager! He was a strong, stalwart man, and suffered no ill effects from his drinking weekends, it would appear. I could never associate this wild, irresponsible young man with the quiet Grandad I knew.

On winter evenings the living room was always hot with large fires he would build up, "putting on a weld" he called it — a phrase from his trade as a boilermaker. There was a large table in the middle of the room, draped in a dark green cloth edged with bobbles. On this would be placed the gramophone, complete with the large horn, and at the side a stack of records, each with a label bearing the picture of a small white dog, head cocked to one side, supposedly listening to "His Master's Voice". Grandad was partial to marches and, after winding the handle of the gramophone, would soon exhaust his collection of John Philip Sousa. While he wound up the machine and played his music, I would prance up and down, with

Granny looking on fondly. As a change she would put a waltz record on the turntable, clutch hold of me, and dance around the room. There was not a lot of space to waltz in, I must admit, but we did our best! She was small and round, and as she danced would pump my arm up and down in time to the music. When she was in a nostalgic frame of mind, she would tell me of when she met Grandad at a dance, when she wore a lovely red flannelette petticoat under her skirt and he had on a new pair of clogs with lots of brass lace-holes. Sometimes he performed his clog-dance for us, rolling back the pegged rug and causing such a clatter on the red and blue tiles.

Grandad had possessed a gramophone once before, but not for very long. He had seen an article in the paper extolling the virtues of a certain gramophone, so he dispatched his order and the money. When it arrived, it turned out to be a very small machine with a cylinder and not a horn, and when it played, a woman's high-pitched voice issued forth. "Squawking" Grandad called it — and other uncomplimentary things — and he couldn't abide it. He returned the machine, plus the cylinder, to the firm that he had bought it from at Rye, and they were kind enough to return his money.

Granny had a large family and there were often relatives visiting us, with lots of talk between the record-playing. Sooner or later, one of them would lure Grandad into playing on one of his tin whistles. He had quite a collection, but my favourite was one which was painted in black and gold diamond patterns. I loved to listen to him playing "Ye banks and braes". Not so my Mother and her sisters when they were small children, for when they heard it on a Saturday night they knew that it heralded their father coming down the street the worse for drink. It held no pleasant association for them.

One aunt who used to visit us was very large, with a voice to match. Everyone who heard her sing would remark on the similarity of her voice to that of Dame Clara Butt, a famous contralto of that era. Certainly it was a powerful voice. This talent was not unique in our family. My mother and her youngest sister also possessed fine singing voices but, unlike their elder sister, they were both sopranos.

Chapter Two

The author aged about three years

From the sweet shop along the main road I bought my halfpenny lucky bags. These sometimes contained a piece of 'locust' which was a kind of fruit, brown and shiny on the outside, crisp and cream-coloured within. There were always a few dolly mixtures and a toffee dab.

When bedtime approached, Granny would bring me a bowl of warm water, soap and a towel. After I had finished washing myself, she would look to see if my neck and ears had been properly attended to, then tuck my long hair behind my ears. I used to loathe this and when she wasn't looking, would pull it back again. I was taught to arrange my clothes neatly in a pile and place them on a chair ready for the next morning. As time passed, it became a habit which I never grew out of. I was then ready to go "up the baulks" — another of Grandad's sayings. Up the steep, dark stairs I went, accompanied by Granny carrying a lighted candle, our only form of illumination. It would flicker in the draught and create eerie shadows on the wall as we mounted the stairs. There was never a handrail and, although this would be dangerous, I never heard of anyone falling from top to bottom! It was taken for granted that you said a prayer before getting into bed; afterwards to be tucked up snug and warm... I always felt as though I was sinking into a lovely nest, for the bed was a feather one. If it was a bad night, with the wind blowing "half a gale" and rain slapping against the window-pane, Granny would say "God bless them as have nowhere to go". Grandad used to tell me that it was "Master Bold" blowing outside if the wind was very strong.

Winter evenings passed one after another, but come the Spring, everything would change. The weather became warmer, and I seemed to spend most of my time outdoors, with a small cousin. There was a large playground close by, and to this we resorted very often to set up shop as our young Auntie Alice directed us. We made our scales from pieces of cardboard, and dug up lumps of clay from which we fashioned tiny loaves and pieces of bacon, slicing the "bacon" with an old blunt knife. For some reason, bits of coloured glass were always available lying about on the ground, and we used these for silver coins. We made do with bits of pottery for pennies. Both my cousin and I were in our element, playing happily, and time meant nothing to us.

Next it was bluebell time, and what wouldn't we do to bring them home to Granny! Alice would take us to the woods, sometimes accompanied by her sweetheart, Arthur. There we would be surrounded by a sea of blue, picking the flowers on their delicate stems until our hands could no longer hold the fragrant bunches, and we were forced to wrap our hankies around the long stems and dangle them by our sides. I have only to smell the scent of bluebells to-day and I am transported back in time to the cool wash-house across the yard, to see Granny filling every available jam-jar with the flowers, until the broad windowsill could hold nothing else.

Later on, this was where Grandad kept his catch after fishing, in a large earthenware bowl lined with yellow glaze, full of fresh water. Into it would go roach, bream and perch, to be fried and relished by all —although the fine bones were always a hazard to me. I must not forget the watercress which was brought home after being plucked from some clear-running stream — unlike to-day's polluted water courses. It always "bit" my tongue, but Granny said that it was very good for you, so down it had to go. Certainly the kind we can buy to-day, with very large leaves, is tasteless in comparison.

Grandad loved to walk for miles into the surrounding countryside, availing himself of whatever was in season. His big red and white "ankisha" (handkerchief) would be full of mushrooms when September came around. One of my favourite dishes was "mushroom dumpling", fastened up in a white floury cloth and steamed. When it was cut open, the mouth-watering gravy would flow onto our plates.

Grandad never returned home without a flower of some description stuck into his buttonhole, even a buttercup or a daisy would do if nothing else was available, and he was never without his walking stick which he had out from the blackthorn bush. I think our passionate love of the countryside is a family trait, and we get the feeling of being trapped if we cannot get into the country as soon as Spring arrives.

It was one of our usual expeditions to the bluebell wood that was almost our undoing, one sparkling day in May. The way we always took led down a narrow lane with deep hedgerows full of wild flowers and hedge parsley that looked like frothy lace. We went over the little stone bridge and passed Cranage watermill — or "Hesketh's" as we called it. The doors always stood open and often the miller would be standing outside, taking a breath of fresh air and covered from head to toe in white flour. Sometimes I would peep inside, to watch the big mill-stones grinding the corn, and hear the great wooden shaft creaking as it slowly rotated and turned the wheels.

We clambered over the stile, crossed the meadow and entered the wood, following the same procedure as usual. This time seemed no different, but we were to have a rude awakening. We walked under the cool shade of the trees, and once more saw the sea of blue around us. The four of us, Auntie Alice, our future Uncle Arthur, my young cousin Frances and myself, sat on a grassy bank to rest and, later, after we had picked our bluebells, we set off for home. By now it was very warm, so Auntie Alice carried her heavy coat over her arm.

We came to an old footbridge which spanned Wincham Brook. It was well worn with age and possessed no hand-rail. Uncle Arthur warned us to be careful because of the poor state it was in, but we had used this short cut home before and were familiar with it. I nipped across first, followed by Auntie Alice, little Frances holding on to her skirt. The inevitable happened. The small child overbalanced, pulling Auntie Alice with her as she fell into the water. Alice was pulled into the reeds by the weight of her coat, and was lying, gently bobbing up and down on her back, with all the bluebells scattered about in the water. My cousin had fallen clear of the reeds into the deeper part of the stream. As I watched, horror stricken, she seemed to be paddling like a little dog towards the mill race. With great presence of mind, Arthur quickly relieved his sweetheart of her heavy coat enabling her to float to the surface of the water. Jumping into the mill stream, he struck out after Frances, catching up with her before she came within the range of the mill-wheel's power. It all happened so quickly. One minute we were all carefree, the next we were in desperate straits.

A man who had been strolling in the meadows came to the water's edge and futilely poked about trying to capture the little girl's bonnet which was floating towards the bank. He couldn't swim, poor man, and seemed to be overcome by what was happening. My cousin was brought back to land again, amazingly no worse for her misadventure, except for a good soaking. It was now Auntie Alice's turn to be rescued; Arthur helped her off her back and out of the water, and we all turned sadly for home. She was wearing a knitted costume which she had made for herself. It was rust coloured with dark green edging (it's amazing how small things stick in one's mind) and was so full of water that the woollen skirt stretched almost down to her toes. What a sight she looked, mud streaming down her face, as Arthur helped her along. She became rather hysterical as we headed for home, crying and laughing in turn, and rubbing the mud from her eyes. Neighbours soon came to our assistance, and while the child was taken to her mother's to be dried out, Granny, very alarmed, rushed to help Alice. She was too upset to chastise us as she would have wanted to do, although she had warned us more than once about crossing the brook. Alice was put to bed to recover from the shock.

I remember the pride we all felt when, later, Arthur received an award for bravery from the Royal Humane Society. The certificate reads, "for having saved two people from drowning". Uncle Arthur had, on another occasion, saved two little boys from drowning in this same brook. One, whose name was Arthur Inglesfield, couldn't have been more than three years of age. Although Uncle Arthur has been dead many years, the framed certificate still has pride of place on the parlour wall.

The street where we lived at Lostock Gralam had a terraced row of sturdy red brick houses standing on either side. They had been built around the 1880s for men employed locally at the newly erected chemical works. A line of tall black railings enclosed allotments at the bottom of the street, a gate in the middle allowing access to them. Grandad had, at some time, planted an apple pippin in his allotment and as the years went by, this grew into a tall, fruitful tree from which many a juicy apple pie was made.

At the time when I lived with my grandparents, a fair sprinkling of Irish families who had came to join their menfolk were among the tenants, and there was an Irish family next door to us.

Our house, like all the others in the street, had three bedrooms, a front parlour, a kitchen with a broom cupboard large enough to walk into and a privy at the bottom of the yard. Here, Grandad kept his maggots for fishing, in a flat 'Bruno' tobacco tin, placed in a niche high up in the wall. The wooden seat of the privy was scrubbed until it was white and cut squares of newspaper hung from a nail behind the door.

There was a wash-house in the yard, too. This contained a boiler and a small grate, in which a fire was lit on washdays. There was no running water laid on for us so that every bucket of water needed for cooking, washing pots and baths was carried across the yard into the house.

The kitchen faced north, making it rather gloomy, but this was offset by a white lace curtain hung at the sash window. When possible glass jars full of flowers, including wild ones, were placed on the window sill. The furniture was plain, some of it home made, with Grandad's large armchair taking pride of place beside the black-leaded grate. There was almost always a bright fire burning there, be it summer or winter. Small wonder that when all the doors were closed in bad weather one soon became drowsy, owing to Grandad's 'stoking up'.

If we were sitting quietly, I would look for pictures in the fire, seeing ogres, witches and princesses and all sorts of characters there. There was always a kettle of water 'singing' on the hob, ready and waiting to make a pot of tea should anyone turn up.

The black horse-hair sofa felt hard and prickly to my bottom, but Granny sat there often, sitting up very straight. I can see her now, a round comfortable, dark-eyed figure with black straight hair severely parted down the middle, wearing gold sleeper earrings. She had very little silver among the dark hair when she died, in spite of all her trials and tribulations.

She invariably wore black, her blouse fastened tight at the neck with a silver brooch, which she treasured. I think that it was a present from my mother. There were few possessions of any worth, so that those she did own she cherished. A long black skirt and a white apron with a frilled edge complete my picture. I used to comb her hair when she found it difficult to raise her arm due to arthritis. It was a little job that I loved to do.

She had a horror of thunder storms, and as soon as there was a flicker of lighting was away to the broom cupboard, where a chair had already been placed. I was told to bring a stool so that I could sit beside her, safe, as she thought, from the storm. How clammy with sweat I would be, because she held me so close to her. I know that she never overcame this feeling of dread which flooded over her as the thunder rolled and crashed, but at least we were unable to see the flashes of lightning in the dark cupboard. When the storm eventually passed over and she felt safe, we would emerge into the daylight once more. Due to the tension within her, she always felt 'fit for nothing' for quite a while afterwards. It's no wonder that I feel alarmed when a thunder storm is imminent, for the feeling has never altogether disappeared.

At the end of the street was a baker's shop which also sold groceries. There were large sacks standing on the floor, which contained Indian corn for poultry as well as pigeon corn. When 'Indicorn' was brought into the house, we would put a handful of it into the hot oven. When ready, it could be heard popping in all directions. It didn't taste sweet like the genuine pop-corn, of course. The owner of the shop made up his own packets of tea, from large chests of loose tea and sugar was also made up in this way. He had a marble slab at the back of the shop with mounds of butter on it, from which he weighed the amount required, slapping it into shape with two butter-pats. Each shop had its own aroma. This one had the smell of newly baked bread ascending above all the other products.

From the sweet shop along the main road, I bought my halfpenny lucky-bags. These sometimes contained a piece of 'locust' which was a kind of fruit, brown and shiny on the outside, crisp and cream coloured within. There were always a few dolly mixtures and a toffee dab — a type of lollipop. I often bought small amounts of tiger nuts, crinkly little brown things which were very chewy and milky once you had bitten into them. The ever popular coloured gob-stoppers were arrayed in the window along with many other sweets, too numerous to mention. It was like an Aladdin's cave to me. The chip shop stood next door and here I went at times with other children for a pennyworth of cold chips that had been left over from lunch-time, or "dinner time" as we knew it.

Walsh's small shop at the end of our particular row of houses was the one that we visited most often. Everything was sold there, from patent medicines to Army surplus blankets. The lady to whom it belonged was always ready to listen to everyone's tale of woe. She had lost a beloved son in the war and was always compassionate to others. Her complexion was pale and she wore her mass of dark brown hair drawn into a bun in the nape of her neck. At least that was the idea, but sooner or later it would escape from its pins and hang lop-sided, nearer to her shoulders than the back of her neck. The jangle of the bell, as Granny opened the door, accompanied by me, my hand in hers, would bring the lady into the shop, peering at us over her metal-rimmed 'specs'. She enjoyed a conversation with Granny, who had a funny little habit while talking of lifting her money up in her hand and letting it clink back again. I don't think she was aware of doing this; it seemed to be a nervous habit, but standing by her side I would listen to the clink, clink of her coins. Auntie Alice has told me that the shoplady had one particular foible — at exactly eleven o'clock each morning, no matter who was waiting to be served, she would go into the back regions of the shop to make herself a cup of Oxo and reappear carrying the beverage plus a cream cracker in her hand. She would dip the biscuit into the Oxo from time to time, enjoying her snack as she recommenced serving a customer. This would be her main-stay until dinner time. There was never a big rush of customers, just a drifting in and out of one and then another. The shop always looked gloomy, dimly lit by its gas mantle, not at all smart, but it seemed to contain most things that folk required. On the back shelves behind the high counter (at least it seemed high to me) stood rows of coloured glass bottles and jars, containing all manner of medical cures. Castor oil, syrup of figs for the bowels (ugh!) and syrup of squills, a lovely shade of violet, for the children's coughs. She would first weigh the cup, or other vessel which the customer brought for the medicine, on the brass scales, subtracting its weight from the total afterwards. Treacle and syrup were also weighed this way.

As for flour, as little as half an ounce was sold for thickening gravy, such were the times. Can you imagine the look of horror on a shopkeeper's face today if you asked for such a small amount! The lady would scoop the flour into a small white cone, having shaped it with a quick flick of her fingers from a square of paper. A tankard of milk stood in a corner of the shop, left there by a local farmer, to be doled out with a tin measure which hung at its side.

Most of the people in the street were gregarious by nature and loved nothing better than to sit on their doorsteps of an evening. The men would comfortably smoke their pipes, the day's work being over, and the women would gossip, knitting or crocheting if they were more industriously inclined. Sometimes, arguments would arise, and even get out of hand, causing much excitement. None of the joys of television for them, but there would always be a friend willing to help if need be.

Our next-door neighbour was a real character. She was tiny in stature and I never remember seeing her without a man's flat cap. Her usual dress was black and reached to her ankles with the inevitable white apron fastened around her waist, and a small grey knitted shawl covering her thin shoulders. When she encountered me, it was always "God bless you, me darlin'", spoken in her strong Irish brogue. She loved children and sometimes would press a silver sixpence into my hand, tears welling up into her eyes — she was very sentimental. This was most acceptable when I was a small child, but I later became quite embarrassed by so much attention when visiting, if I chanced to meet her. Even so, I look back and remember her generous nature.

In winter she would sometimes hold a 'Tater-pie Supper', baking a meat and potato pie in a very large enamelled bowl, stoking up the kitchen fire to get the oven hot for baking.

All and sundry would be invited to these "do's". She liked her beer on these occasions, and a tall lanky youth willingly undertook to run errands to the local off-licence for her and her husband. Friends would gather around in her front parlour and as the evening progressed, so would her nostalgic frame of mind. Irish ballads would be sung, with our neighbour starting off, her friends joining in the choruses. I have heard her singing songs like "I'll take you home again Kathleen", "Eileen Allana", and watched the tears rolling down her cheeks, making a sad picture. I think she loved a good cry now and again, for soon all would be well and she would be doing an Irish jig.

One of her famous 'Tater-pie Suppers' had a rather different ending on one occasion. The large pie had been baked as usual in the kitchen oven and set upon a table. Children were attracted like flies around a honey pot if anything was going on, and on this evening Willa must have been feeling more magnanimous than ever, for she said to the girl left in charge of the mouth-watering pie, "Help them children to this pie", and went to join the adults in the other room. Much later, when they returned to the kitchen for their super, there was very little potato pie left, for she had been taken literally. I don't know what the outcome was for I was not present, but the tale of the pie's disappearance was related to first one and then another with much amusement.

Sometimes, an old man would be seen and heard in the street playing his barrel organ or hurdy-gurdy, laboriously turning the handle and churning out a tune. This would cause a bit of a diversion for the small children playing around, who would be quite entertained by it.

Across the road from where we lived, there were two men employed by the old firm of Brunner and working at the Winnington works on the other side of town. Granny told me when I was older that hail, rain or snow they would set out to walk to their destination, wearing sturdy clogs, to be at work for the early shift at six o'clock, returning by the same way after their day's work was done. Such things were not unusual. Hard times, indeed, but they at least had a job to go to.

Chapter Three

Grandparents: Samuel and Frances Hitchen

Grandad was once sent to the butcher's to buy a sheep's head, a chore he was unused to performing. When the shopkeeper began to wrap it up in paper, Grandad said to him: "Tek his eyes out and then he wunna know where he's going."

We were a pretty robust family, due, I am sure, to the good plain food set before us and to Granny's 'fathoming out' for us, as she called it. I must say that I could not now do justice to some of the different foods I enjoyed as a child. It seems that the eating habits of the working class have altered considerably.

Granny often bought half a sheep's head from the butcher; I don't think that it cost above a few coppers (nothing ever did, it seems). She would soak it in salt water for a few hours, then prepare it for the pan, boiling it until the meat fell from the bones and she would add all manner of vegetables to the liquid. It made delicious broth and I liked to see the twinkling bits of gold sailing on the surface.

There were the usual cow heels, pigs' trotters, tripe, black puddings with lots of fat in them, and cows' udder which could be bought ready cooked and sliced accordingly for sandwiches. Savoury ducks cost less than a penny each.

Grandad was once sent to the butcher's to buy a sheep's head, a chore he was unused to performing. When the shopkeeper began to wrap it up in paper, Grandad said to him "Tek his eyes out and then he wunna know where he's going". It was his way of telling the butcher that he should have known better. His very dry sense of humour had people in stitches, although he didn't set out to amuse. He was very well known in this area and sometimes beyond, for his comical sayings. He never thought them up, they just came out spontaneously, but the community appreciated them and would recall many of them long after he had gone.

Granny had a very light touch with pastry and when she made a rabbit pie, the crust was the crowning glory. I have never tasted any since that compared with hers. The rabbits usually cost sixpence, but the skins were sold to the rag and bone man for twopence each — to be sold in turn to the manufacturers for making fur gloves and so on.

Blue moulds were exchanged by him for a few rags, too. These were pale chalky blue bricks which were used to clean the hearth, making it look white and smooth. There were 'donkey stones' from the same source, but these were harder and brown in colour, more often than not used to clean the back-door step; the blue moulds were used on the front-door steps.

I used to watch Granny chopping fresh mint which smelled lovely: she showed me as I grew a bit older how to do this little task neatly and nimbly, chopping through the pile of fresh mint until the juice oozed out and the scent of it pervaded the kitchen.

We were never without fresh food. The fishmonger called with his horse and cart and sometimes Granny bought finnon haddock, a great favourite (and not bright yellow as it's sometimes coloured to-day), from him. Now and again he would sell to her, for next to nothing, a large cod's head. There was always enough fish on it to make a couple of nice steaks. Grandad maintained that this part of the fish was the most nourishing and who were we to disagree? Fresh mussels were bought from the fishmonger too, measured out into our large basin, afterwards to be boiled over the kitchen fire in the ever ready black iron pan. When they were cool, I helped to winkle them from out of their navy-blue shells onto a large dish. I forget the cost of them, but I have been told that juicy kippers were a halfpenny a pair!

Buttermilk was a favourite of mine, brought to the door by the farmer. It stood on the milk-float alongside a tankard of fresh milk. We used a big earthenware jug for this and it was filled to the brim for three pence. Grandad was partial to mashing his boiled potatoes in buttermilk. It was a common saying that buttermilk put a lining on your stomach. Perhaps it did, for we didn't suffer from indigestion.

According to Aunty Alice, a dumpy little figure used to be seen walking down the street every Friday. It was the shrimp woman, wearing a white apron over her clothes, and carrying a large wide basket over her arm. When anyone went out to her, she would invariably ask, "Which ones dy'a want, pick't uns or t'others?". Alice always chose the peeled shrimps, sixpenny worth. If you bought those with the shells on, you got a bigger quantity, but you had to remove the shells, so you were not much better off. She travelled by train all the way from Widnes to sell her wares on a Friday, staying in the street long enough to have a meal at our Irish neighbour's house.

In Grandad's mushrooming days, there was one occasion in particular which was a bit of a disaster. He had been searching for mushrooms and had at last filled his red and white handkerchief to capacity. Setting off for home across a meadow, he chanced to meet the farmer who stopped him and said, "D'ye know you're on private ground?" Knowing every inch of the public footpaths and rights of way, Grandad replied that he was breaking no law. The farmer then said, "Give me them", pointing to the mushrooms. "I winna", said Grandad. "Then give me half", said the other. "I winna give thee half and if tha doesn't be off I'll wipe thee nose with this stick". At that the farmer just walked away and Grandad continued on his way home.

Worse was yet to come, as he walked across the next field, a bull began to chase him. Just managing to scramble to safety through a hedge, scratched and torn, he stood at the other side triumphantly and said out loud to the bull, "Now thee can fetch thee Grandfeether", for his temper was really aroused by all these goings on. Poor Grandad, and what a day! Later he was to say, "I feel as though I've been pulled from Lymm to Warburton". This was a well known local saying when a person felt worn out and bedraggled, and it arose from a legend about these Cheshire villages. In mediaeval times, if anyone committed an offence or misdemeanour they were tied to a hurdle and drawn by a horse, bumpety, bump, from the church in one village to the parish church, about two miles away, in the other, and back again.

When mushrooms were being prepared for a dumpling, Grandad used to say "Dunna throw the peelings away", then he would put them in a small bowl, cover with boiling water, and place them in the oven. After they had stewed a while, he would strain off the liquid, stir in a little seasoning and drink it. He was very sure that it did him good.

I liked to watch him thrust the poker into the fire and when it was red-hot, plunge it into his tankard of beer, making it fizz up until the foam almost came over the top. He always added a bit of nutmeg and sugar before drinking it.

When I was well turned four years of age, I began attending the local infant school. I believe that Granny took me on my first day. Pictures flash through my mind of the little black and white school and its staff, and Granny's advice to me, "Always try and do your best". I was to attend here for two short periods, leaving for a while when my mother married again.

We had two sisters on the staff, aptly named by the children "big Miss Blower" and "little Miss Blower". The description speaks for itself, but my favourite was the smaller one, who took us for religious knowledge, or 'scripture' as it was then called. I was given stamps with perforated edges and biblical pictures printed on them, and an album to stick them in, for being good at "answering". We also received these stamps at Sunday School at the local chapel.

We had to be quiet in the cloakroom, before entering classes. On one occasion, I created a disturbance by chasing another little girl in and out of the clothes racks. We were laughing excitedly when a teacher saw us, and as I was the culprit I was sent to stand in front of the headmistress. I was near to panic as I walked through the bead curtains which hung across the opening to her small office, the glass beads jingling as I disturbed them. I remember standing before her desk, anxiously waiting for her to stop writing and to look up at me. I expected at least to be told off, if not smacked, but when I told her what I had been up to, all she said was "Don't be noisy in future. You may go now". She must have taken pity on a startled child. It's amazing how so small an incident can affect a child, because for a long while afterwards I never saw bead curtains but I was reminded of being "sent for".

During the dark winter evenings, Granny kept herself occupied by making hearth-rugs among other things. The cloth which she used came from various sources. There were cast-off skirts and coats from the family, beside suitable bits and pieces from neighbours, the more colourful the better. To start with, there would be a heap of oddments at one side, and once the snipping started, another pile of neat small strips of material at the other. It was my job to hand Granny the colours she required from these. I would wait, inwardly impatient, to see the heap diminish. Potato sacks, thoroughly scrubbed beforehand on the yard, were the foundation for these rugs; a sharpened wooden clothes-peg the tool, which became quite polished with use. They were warm and cosy to the feet, bright and cheerful to look upon and cost literally nothing except the time and work involved.

Another 'home industry' was the making of patchwork quilts. This was much more to my liking than pegged rugs! The neighbour adjoining our house on the other side was a dressmaker, who would sell Granny bundles of material left over from her cutting out. Patiently, she converted these into patchwork quilts, backing them with pieces of blanket that still had plenty of wear in them, which made them very warm when spread over the bed. I had the tiny pieces of leftovers and sewed them, if that is the right description, up into doll's clothes. Actually, I never cared for sewing even when I grew up, but I am pleased my two daughters differ from me in this respect.

Speaking of toys, one of my earliest possessions was a teddy bear that an uncle had bought me. It was rather large for me to handle at first and my mother said that I didn't much care for his large glass eyes, which seemed to stare and stare at me. In time, however, he became my favourite toy and I grew to love him. He is present on various photos, sitting beside me when I was aged about three or four years old. Mother repaired the pads on his hands and feet, as the years went by, when his stuffing started to poke through. I gave him away to a cousin of mine when I grew up, and felt instantly deprived!

Another toy that I was fond of playing with was a very small wicker-work doll's pram with tiny iron wheels. I never pushed it but would trundle it behind me, pulling it up the steps between the kitchen and parlour, an obstacle which I had to negotiate. In reality it was only a shallow step.

Mother kept me looking very smart and would often bring me something new to wear when she came home from Manchester on her days off. Sometimes it may only have been hair ribbons, but these were quite expensive in comparison to other items, some of them being wide taffeta ones in various coloured check. They lasted for years, and when I was young I wore them in my hair, where they sat looking like large butterflies. When I look at old photos, I am struck by the fact that some of my dresses look quite modern, with their box pleats and design.

Gaiters, or leggings, were fashionable at that time and I had both calf-leather and thick stockinette ones. They were very warm and came up over my knees. Fastening them was the problem; they had hundreds of buttons down each side, at least when they were being fastened with the steel button-hook, I felt this was so! Many's the time that I have squawked and squeaked as a bit of my fat, chubby leg was pinched between the button and button-hook, especially if the person performing this task was in a hurry. The said button-hook was rather unusual in that it had a spring-like action, which enabled it to be folded up into a small compass, easy to carry in a handbag. My eldest daughter now has it in her school museum!

Chapter Four

Parents: Mr and Mrs James Cloudsdale with the author (left) and baby sister Edith (right).

On an Easter Sunday in March my sister was born. The lovely woollen shawl that I thought was mine was switched away to wrap the new baby in. My nose was quite put out of joint and I remember feeling rather peeved.

Our village of Lostock Gralam was split into two parts known as 'top' and 'bottom'. The infant school was situated at the foot of the canal bridge, 'th'accaduct' as it was popularly named, because the canal is carried over Wincham Brook at this point. The large corn mill adjoining the canal bank is now obsolete and the place is used for gardening and farming equipment. Here, Clement, a small boy from our part of the village, wandered down to the canal and was drowned.

Our annual Rose Fête was held in a meadow next to the senior school, and apart from there being a Rose Queen and the usual dancing troupes, fair and so on, there was a large sports event, including cycle and track racing. This attracted crowds of people from all around. As the years went by less interest was taken in the Fête for various reasons, but the times that I recall were full of excitement, reaching fever pitch as 'The Day' drew near. My favourite was the Maypole Dance. How I loved to watch as the boys bowed to their partners when the band struck up, and, setting off holding the brightly-coloured ribbons, wove their intricate patterns. I would watch the top of the maypole with bated breath where the basketwork design was appearing and wonder how on earth the children were going to reverse it without becoming entangled. It was a great relief to me when all was completed safely.

I felt most proud on one occasion as I watched my cousin, Sam, dressed in his Morris dancing outfit, marching in the procession, which wended its way along the main road. The pavements were thronged with people as it passed by, clapping and participating in the happy atmosphere around them. Sam was dressed in white shirt and trousers, with coloured ribbons criss-crossed around his legs, and from time to time would shake the ruffles that he held in his hands to make the bells jingle.

Once, I was chosen to take part in the festivities, along with five other little girls. We wore white, frilly voile dresses (mine being made by the lady next door to us) and white plimsolls with the inevitable bells attached. We were called the Fairy Bells. Soon it was our turn to ascend the dais, watched by the

Rose Queen and crowds of people. The band began to play the tune "St. Patrick's Day" — I've always remembered it — and we were off, galloping hand in hand around the boards. "Fairy Bells"? Well, never mind, we received lots of applause as we filed off at the finish.

I cannot write about Fête days without mentioning a special one, Royal Knutsford May Day. The royal prefix was used because Queen Victoria was supposed to have paid a visit there on one occasion. Knutsford, as most people know, was Mrs. Gaskell's 'Cranford', and is only a few miles from my home. It was the *'piece de resistance'* of May Day celebrations, people travelling from many miles away to attend. I must have been quite small when Granny and Grandad took me for the first time, travelling by train on the old Cheshire Line, squeezed in like sardines, cheek by jowl, some passengers even standing. The May Queen's house was always swathed in garlands of flowers, everywhere around being full of colour. In all the beautiful procession, my favourite character for same reason was 'The Man in the Green'! This was a man dressed overall in masses of foliage, peering through the greenery, twirling and cavorting as he progressed along the road. I was always enthralled by this character, who attracted me more than the May Queen.

Mother's older sisters told of previous May Days at the turn of the century. The young farm labourers would turn up, having saved money all the year round from their meagre wages for the sole purpose of enjoying this special day off from work. Of course the girls were allowed the day off too, from service, and a hilarious time was had by everyone by all accounts. I remember one particular fête day. Granny and I sat in the cobbled yard of a black and white thatched inn, the White Bear, where Grandad had deposited us while he went inside for a drink. Shortly, he came out to join us accompanied by a gentleman who looked to be quite old. He talked to my grandparents, the conversation going above my head. I remember also that he placed one hand on each side of my forehead and then felt various bones in my head, passing remarks to my grandparents. I hadn't a clue what all this was about, but later Granny told the family with pride, and also the neighbours, that I was a clever child and would go far according to this gentleman who was, I presume, a phrenologist. Alas, his predictions have not come true, for I have not moved far!!

There was an aunt who was a year or two older than Alice, working in domestic service, who was possessed of a kind but also impulsive nature and when she was out of a job would return home from time to time. Arguments with her sister would usually bring forth from Grandad, "You should be a thousand miles apart!" I remember watching her stand before a large gilt-edged mirror which hung over the parlour mantelpiece, fluffing or frizzing out her thick dark hair with finger and thumb until she resembled a Zulu warrior! Granny caught me on one occasion trying to do the same and threatened to bring a pair of scissors to cut off the hair that was full of knots or 'lugs', making it almost impossible to comb out properly.

About this time a dance which came over from America was very popular: it was the 'Maxina' and when my two young aunts were feeling amicable towards one another, they would play this record endlessly, concocting their own version of the dance as they went along. When I was a schoolgirl, another dance originating in America swept the country. This was the 'Charleston', and we would be kicking our heels up performing this dance even on our way to school, such was the craze.

Our home scene would never be complete without Grandad's wood, reared up in one corner of the front room; choice pieces, which he kept there for making his fishing rods. They were a work of art and he even made the brass ferules that kept the partings together. He was a boilermaker by trade, but also a very good carpenter. His ancestors were farmers and wheelwrights, generations of them, who hailed from Barrow near Chester, and as a lad he had helped his grandfather and uncles on their farm. I have heard him say that many tools were used in the intricate work of making a cart-wheel.

He was probably brought up to take great care of tools, for it was woe betide anyone who touched his. There was a length of canvas with little pockets sewn inside to hold his small tools and the big wooden needles which he used for making his fishing nets. It was usually lying on a table in the front room along with his other 'trantliments' as he called them. He invariably knew if anything had been touched or tampered with and I thought this was magic.

Once, he made a replica of one of his fishing rods, a delightful little object which I used on two or three occasions when he allowed me to accompany him on fishing expeditions near home. Picture, if you will, an elderly man and a little girl holding a fishing rod apiece, sitting on the banks of the brook which meandered through Nobby Griffiths' fields till it disappeared under the road and into what is now the ICI works. Silence would reign more often than not, for Grandad was hard of hearing, being a boiler-maker. If I did have anything to say he would cup his ear with his big hand and bend down to listen. I never caught any fish but I got much pleasure from sitting there beside him. He brought two pieces of cork along for us to sit upon and a large black umbrella in case of rain. I wish that my small fishing rod had not been lost for my young grandson would have appreciated it, I am sure.

Returning to the parlour, metaphorically speaking, in summer there was usually a wasps' nest laid out neatly on a piece of newspaper on the table, by Grandad. This habit of his always annoyed Granny and, worse still, his habit of plucking young wasps just hatched, from their waxy homes and throwing them out through the open front door, while busily preparing his wasps' grub bait for the next fishing expedition. There came a time when someone was stung as they white-stoned the step and after the commotion had settled down, Grandad was berated by Granny who gave him 'the length of her tongue' ending with, "What have I told thee Sam, about that trick. If I've told thee once, I've told thee a hundred times!"

He acquired his wasps' nests or 'cakes' on his country rambles, watching the hedgerows where there was plenty of activity. After locating the nest he would push an oily rag down the hole, light it, then seal the entrance with a clod of earth. 'Smoking them out', he described the operation. After a while he used his small shovel to open up the nest and carefully remove the 'cakes', which were sometimes as large as a dinner plate.

The object which took my fancy when he was making a fishing rod was his tiny iron glue pot, which had inside of it a still smaller pot. The outer one contained water, while the other held pieces of glue which was bought in a solid state, looking like brittle pieces of toffee. When I held them up to the light they were almost transparent and glowed in a shade of yellow. The utensils and the glue were placed at the side of the fire, where the water surrounding the tiny pot soon reached boiling point, melting the glue inside. It was quite a delicate performance getting everything ready for finishing off his fishing rods. The large balls of string lying around were used for making the keep-nets. Watching him make these I noticed how large and strong his hands were with big thumb joints, yet he handled the wooden needle and string very deftly.

While getting along with his hobby, he would sometimes mention a bit of family history. His grandparents had been farmers and wheelwrights from Barrow, although his parents lived at Northwich, where he was born. They had had a smallholding along Manchester Road, before the railway came to the town, and Grandad said that when he was a 'nipper' he was given the task of bringing the cows up at milking time. There was a tall oak tree with a seat around it at the crossways, which is now a busy thoroughfare with traffic lights at the bottom of Station Bridge. A five-barred gate led into meadows surrounding Witton Church and through this he would go for the cattle. It is hard for me to visualise this pastoral scene today when the town has altered so much. When Grandad married he took his young bride to live there with his parents (he was the youngest of a family of four children), but today there is no sign left of the smallholding, just a long row of terraced houses.

Time passed pleasantly by, and one day Mother took me to visit her recently married brother. I didn't realise at the time that the dark curly-haired young man who was present was to become my new father. He had been demobbed after serving as a very young man on the Western Front, and was visiting his sister. As it turned out it was a very close relationship, for she had married my mother's brother. We went to visit my uncle and his wife quite often after that. It gave my mother the chance to see the young brother-in-law and vice versa!

Eventually, we visited Dad's parents, who were kind to us from the beginning. I remember there being a small rocking chair in the kitchen, that had a red paisley cushion on its seat. I was allowed to sit in it and I did so very often, rocking myself back and forth. It appealed to me because it was just the right size and I was oblivious to those around me so long as I could rock to and fro in it.

When my Mother got married I left Granny's, where my home had always been, with mixed feelings — on the one hand, sad at leaving those I loved; on the other, looking forward to a new home and a new father. Actually, it was a case of exchanging one set of grandparents for another, because we went to live with Dad's people.

The picture that springs to mind regarding the new Grandma is of her in the outside wash-house swathed in steam and up to her elbows in soap suds. Most of her time was spent there (or so it seemed to me), poor soul; she was very hard-working and although she had a family of her own to look after she still found room for us. She baked the most lovely bread and there was often a bowl of dough standing in the hearth, rising under a tea-cloth. There were few houses available at that time for young married couples of the working class, and probably the majority of them began their married lives in lodgings, with strangers, if their families could not, or would not, accommodate them.

My new father was working at Appleton's, the brick works, but, before long, he heard that a large steel manufacturers, Sommers of Shotton, were requiring men. Although this place was the other side of Chester, nothing daunted, he decided to apply for a job, as the wages were much better. In the event, it was I who accompanied him to Chester and beyond. We travelled on his bike, with me sitting on a plump cushion which was strapped to the cross-bar. Comfortable, that is until we found ourselves riding on rough roads for mile after mile.

At last we arrived at our destination, and this huge works,

as it was then, took on the aspect of a big town. Dad set me down at the entrance and gave me strict orders not to move until he returned, and I watched with anxious eyes as he disappeared from view. I must have looked worried as the minutes ticked by, because a works 'Bobby' came to reassure me, giving me a silver sixpence. I kept the small coin for a long while. Dad came along shortly after, smiling broadly. He had landed a job. We returned home rapidly, only stopping to buy some apples from a farm on the way.

Dad found us accommodation at Shotton just over the border into Wales, and we packed up and followed him when he started his new job. The house we lived in was a terraced one, situated in a cul-de-sac with high boards across the end. There were knot-holes in the wood through which I peeped and saw the sands of the Dee stretched out before me for miles. I remember little else about this period of my life, except the lady's name where we lodged. It was Mrs Baskett!!

Dad had quite a decent job at the steelworks and, after a while, he was offered a house. For a time, all was well, Then somehow things started to go wrong. Men who were already members of a Union began to gang up against Dad because he wouldn't join one. He could be stubborn when he wished, so the more these men got at him, the more he refused to comply with them. Eventually they 'sent him to Coventry' but nevertheless he stuck it out and continued to do his work well. Then came a bigger problem, for Mother was now pregnant and began to feel home-sick. As time wore on she got worse and worse until Dad gave up in despair and we returned to our own folks. One would have thought that the promise of a house was enough to overcome this nostalgia, but with mother it was not. But Dad was now without a job!

Luckily, it wasn't long before things began looking up from the point of view of employment. The local chemical works began taking on extra men and Dad was offered a job. We lodged with Dad's parents once again and, on an Easter Sunday in March, my sister was born. The lovely woollen shawl that I thought was mine was switched away to wrap the new baby in. My nose was quite put out of joint, as the saying goes, when taken to view the new baby, for there it lay, wrapped up snugly in 'the shawl'. I remember feeling quite peeved. No warning had been given to me that I was about to acquire either a brother or a sister. I don't think that psychology was thought about much in those days. The bedroom where mother lay with her new baby was rather cold and damp, and although one son was now married and living elsewhere, this was the only bedroom available. Grandma had done the best she could for us.

When Mother was up and about, Dad realised that he would have to look around for a new place for us and, quite soon, he found one. The house we went to live in was quite roomy (no trouble in that quarter) but as is often the way another obstacle was in the offing. We were once again in lodgings, the family who owned the house having two young children plus a baby a couple of months older than ours. I'm sorry to say that our baby cried quite often in the day-time, but was even worse at night. The landlady complained about the nuisance. Mother replied that she was doing her best to keep our baby quiet. She helped the lady with her laundry and assisted her in many ways with the chores, 'holding the candle to the light' as the saying goes.

The last straw came when I quarrelled with the child next door. The upshot of it all was that my parents decided to send me back to live with my own grandparents until they had a house of their own. I was uprooted yet again. What mattered most, though, was that I was welcomed with open arms by Granny and Grandad. My young Aunt Alice was living at home now and I shared her room and bed. It was now her turn to see me safely up the steep stairs and snuff out the candle. I was in seventh heaven, oblivious to poor Mother and Dad struggling with a fretful baby in someone else's home.

There were certain objects that gave me pleasure at Granny's, ordinary everyday things, but delightful to me as a child. One such object was a picture which hung in our bedroom. It was a painting of a girl crouching beside a pond, hands outstretched towards several fluffy yellow ducklings. She had long flaxen hair tied back with a blue ribbon, a lovely smile, and wore a lace pinafore over her dress. I always thought that it was my cousin Molly, it was so like her. I never mentioned it to anyone, but took this for granted.

There was an old desk which had been in the family for years that took my interest. When opened up, it revealed what appeared to be three books standing in the centre. Actually they were just imitations, and when pulled out it was obvious that they were really hollow receptacles. I loved the secrecy of it all, and could never resist peeping inside to see if any treasure had been placed there, but I never found any! Another piece of furniture I was drawn to like a magnet was a large wooden blanket chest. It also had a secret compartment, a narrow, shallow drawer which slid out in a semi-circle if one pushed in the right place. All I ever found — and I looked many times — were bobbins of cotton. So much for hidden treasure! Victorians so loved secrets, even in their furniture.

Chapter Five

Rudheath C of E School in about 1926 with teacher Mr R P Porter. The author is in the second row down, third from the left.

One day a teacher caught me reading a naive and innocent note a boy had written me: she commanded me to stand in front of the class and read it out loud. As I passed the open fireplace I dropped it into the flames and she accused me of being too big for my shoes.

*A*lice and Arthur were now courting in earnest. He worked on a farm not far from his home and, when they were married, I sometimes accompanied my Aunt Alice when she took a parcel of sandwiches and a can of tea to him, during his break from ploughing the fields. One of his horses was huge and black and answered to the name of 'Captain'. Although he was so big he had a very placid nature, and if I was lucky, I was allowed to ride on his back for a short distance. As he lumbered along, the brasses that hung down his massive chest clinked together most pleasantly. Later, we would return home down the narrow lane and over the canal bridge.

The local council was then busy on an important project, a new housing estate at Rudheath for the working-class. I believe ours was one of the first to be built in this area after the First World War, among green fields and trees. As soon as one house was completed, it was put on show to the public, a novel experience for this time.

"If only we could have a home of our own," Mother had said to Dad. They had had their name put down on the waiting list and waited patiently for their turn. It seemed a prize out of their reach and they could hardly believe their luck when the tide turned in their favour and the miracle happened. At last they were allocated a home of their own, a place where they could bring up children without pressures from anyone. It didn't take long for them to be installed, from what my mother has told me, for they possessed very little in the way of furniture, having been in lodgings. Dad spread a rug on the kitchen floor, set the baby on it and said, "Now you can damn well cry as much as you like," or words to that effect! The strange thing was, she never did cry and was a different child from then on.

The estate was built in a rural setting, with gardens adjoining a field where, as summer progressed, mowing grass grew tall and we would watch the farm workers cut and gather it in at harvest time. There was a tall ash tree beside a deep pit or pond in this field, which made a delightful sound on a breezy day. If you closed your eyes you could imagine that you were by the sea-shore; the sound it made as the wind rustled through its branches was exactly like waves rolling in. I often played at the foot of this tree, plaiting small cradles from the reeds at the pond's edge and placing a carefully chosen daisy or buttercup within, as a substitute for a baby. This was a favourite pastime of small girls and I was quite happy to be alone as I played.

There was always an element of risk when we entered the fields around, because the farmer who rented them was noted for his crotchety temper. He would ride down on his old 'bike' from the farm and woe betide any of us caught trespassing. He was only small in stature but he could certainly put fear into us when we saw him approaching and we would scuttle off pretty smartly! Having said that, lads still went bird-nesting along the hedgerows, and the girls still 'got in' to pick wild flowers. He was the bane of our lives but you could probably say that the situation was reciprocated!

This same farmer delivered milk in the morning with a horse and float. The cart was built on two wheels, so that it almost touched the ground when the milk tankard was full, and when he stood at the front holding the reins we called it his chariot! If you visited the farm during the afternoon, you would find that the milk float was the temporary abode of a host of fowl who cackled and flew up in all directions when anyone approached.

The roads were not finished when we moved into our house. I would stand at the gate to watch the big steam-roller huffing and puffing as it went past, crushing the stones and levelling the road ready for tarmacing the surface.

Mother was always telling me to pick my feet up properly. I always seemed to catch my toes on something or other and often had a sore knee bandaged up. On one occasion, while running across the road, I tripped up on the jagged stones, piercing my hand badly. I still have a small scar to this day to remind me of the accident.

Dad was settled nicely in his job at the chemical works, travelling to and fro on his bicycle, his hours of work being from 7.30am until 5pm. When the days grew shorter and it was dark before he came home, he used an acetylene lamp to light his way. It was similar to a small metal box to look at, with a little glass door at the front, and it was quite a ritual to get it lit. First of all, Dad would unscrew the receptacle which was attached to the underside, place inside it a few pieces of carbide and add to it a small amount of water. Having screwed it together again, he opened the little glass door and put a lighted match inside, and a little blue flame would shoot up from the hole in the bottom of the lamp. This would cast a bright light when it started to burn steadily, and would glow crimson through the tiny coloured windows at each side. If there was insufficient carbide in the lamp, the flame would sink lower and lower until it flickered out, so it was too bad if you were riding home in the dark — it was a case of dismounting from your cycle and walking the rest of the way home!

Little by little Mother and Dad provided us with a cosy and attractive home. They often attended local sales where furniture was being auctioned. We acquired four lovely dining chairs in this way, then later a wall-clock which had a most melodious chime as it sang out the hours. Mother made cretonne covers for the chairs, and polished the legs until they shone, covering them with old woollen stockings from which the feet had been cut to protect them from our shoes!

Saturday morning was set aside for cleaning the flues and blackleading the kitchen grate. 'Zebra' grate polish was a black powder which when mixed with a small amount of water and applied with a small brush (not forgetting the 'elbow grease' required) would bring a shine to the iron grate which you could 'see your face through', according to Mother. All this hard work was accomplished while we children were still in bed. When we did arrive downstairs, all the black soot and mess had disappeared leaving a clean, comfortable kitchen. The oven was then all set for the week-end baking session, and reached quite a high temperature as coals were piled on the fire. As this procedure carried on into summer, regardless, the door always stood open for fresh air.

Before Dad became a shift-worker and was still on 'days', he always took it upon himself to cook our Sunday breakfast. He had served as a batman to some officer during the war and was quite expert, so Sunday mornings were something we all looked forward to.

When my sister was old enough to share my bed we slept in a bedroom which had a small fireplace in it. It was so cheerful and warm on winter evenings to watch the flames flickering, making shadows on the wall. I would amuse my young sister by making little moving pictures of rabbits and dogs by putting my hands together and twiddling my fingers about. She was fond of this amusement. True, every bucket of coal the fire required had to be carried upstairs by our parents, and the cinders cleaned from the grate the next day. We also used a fire-brick, wrapped in an old piece of flannelette, to keep our feet warm in bed. This brick was kept in the oven when no cooking activity was going on, so it was usually very warm. Sometimes we used an oven-shelf, wrapped up just like the brick, but this went cool much quicker.

Granny and Grandad visited us from time to time, pleased that we now had a home of our own. Grandad enjoyed doing a bit of carpentry for us. Among other things, he made a stool each for my sister and me, an attractive plant-stand for my mother and, because Dad was fond of gardening, he made him a wheelbarrow, which I believe was quite a tricky object to construct. When we first went to live in the new house, Grandad planted a sprig from an elder-bush close to the back door, and as we grew so did the elder-tree. It became very tall, and when later I was enthralled by the tales of Robin Hood, I used some of its branches to make long bows and fancied myself as an archer!

I was now attending St John's Infant School, a small red brick building that stood beside the main road, which was much quieter than it is today. We used to saunter along to school passing the pits or ponds which abounded hereabouts. One was larger than most and covered in a slimy green algae, which gave it a dark mysterious appearance. It was used by some of the children's mothers as a warning and they would say, "If you don't behave, Ginny Greenteeth'll get you". I always felt uneasy when passing this pit, never lingering here. There was an old woman who frequented this area. Small and stout, dressed in black, her thick gathered skirts reaching to her toes, she wore a coloured handkerchief over her head which was tied under her chin and a short black cape covering her shoulders. We called her 'Nanny Chew-Tobacco' because of her habit of smoking an old black pipe. Her nose was bulbous and her complexion red, due no doubt to the hours she spent outdoors. We dreaded meeting her along the road for the boys would call after her and she would chase everybody within range, although no-one was ever caught. I believe that she was one of those people who loved to be on the road, wandering about, but she always returned to the town's 'Workhouse' for a night's shelter. This went on for years then suddenly we missed her and it was said that she had died.

At church festivals the curate held a service for us, it being a Church of England school. There was a tiny chapel attached to the end of the school building which was revealed when the teachers drew back the sliding partition. It was complete with altar, candlesticks, cross, and so on. There may have been other schools similarly equipped, but I have never seen any. It is now demolished, replaced by a row of six houses. When I became the monitor in my class, helping the teacher by keeping the cupboards tidy among other chores, she would reward me on holidays by giving me the flowers from the window-sill, which I couldn't wait to present to my mother. "Close your eyes and hold out your hands," I would say to her, which obligingly she would do, feigning surprise each time this happened. When I left home for school each day I would wave to her until I reached the corner down the road almost falling over backwards.

I was sorry to leave the little school when it was time for me to 'go up' to the big one. It catered for infants and also for children up to school leaving age, which was then fourteen. Soon I went into the same class as an older cousin. Children were 'put up' according to their ability and sometimes found themselves in a class with much older pupils.

Rudheath C of E School which I left when I was fourteen, as all the children did except for those who passed the entrance exam to the 'Grammar School', was a red brick Victorian building with a house attached, built in 1841. Previously occupied by various headmasters, a local family now lived there with six children, the youngest being a girl, who often leant against the little gate adjoining the boys' playground, watching us march around in circles doing our drills — "arms up, arms outstretched, arms down", the sum total of our PE. Our headmaster at that time was a good teacher but could be very stern. He would use what we called a pointer for this purpose, which was a thick wooden stick tapered at the end for pointing at writing on the blackboard. Slaps with this instrument on the open palms could be painful indeed, but, barring one or two exceptions, were usually received stoically by the boys.

There was one teacher whom we liked very much, with a good sense of humour. He taught both standards four and five at one stage of his career, and we were sorry when he left with his family for Canada. We were not to know that after a couple of years he would return and become our head teacher.

The school was heated by a big iron stove in which coke was used, and the headmaster sat next to it at his high desk. There was also a large open fireplace, surrounded by a brass-rimmed fireguard, where fires were lit in winter. Sometimes I was lucky enough to sit at the end of a long desk next to it, which was cosy and warm and, if we were extremely quiet, sometimes a mouse would come creeping out of its little hole and move quickly around the hearth rustling back the same way it had come, by which time I would be ready to fly to the other side of the class! Our large schoolroom was divided into two sections by a wooden and glass partition, which could be folded back when necessary, and classes were held on either side. It was rather a tight squeeze, but we managed.

When the teacher who went to Canada returned with his family, he took over from our old headmaster, and his way of teaching and running the school was quite different. His was a less strict approach altogether and much more relaxed. Children still received the cane when he thought it was justified but he was more flexible in his dealings with the school in general. He had served as an Army Captain in the First World War and would tell us little anecdotes of a humorous kind that would have us falling about laughing. This suited us to a 'T', as it made a change from serious routine. He once told us that he had failed his entrance exam to the Grammar School as a boy and that his father had paid the fee for a place for him. He later went to college and became a teacher like his father and his brothers. He told us this to encourage us. "Do not despair if you fail the first time, but keep on trying," he would say. Sometimes children put in for the scholarship exam would be more worried if they should pass than if they should fail, wondering where their parents would find the money for their special uniforms and books. Of course some families were better off, but I think it's fair to say that the majority of parents found it a struggle to keep up a decent standard of living for their offspring in those days.

My sister and I never went short of the necessities of life, there only being the two of us, but there were not as many luxuries to be had as is the case with children to-day. On the other hand, it made us more appreciative of what our parents did for us.

In our school we were given two important pieces of information about our local history, the first being that the road running past Rudheath Church to Middlewich was a Roman one (it does run as straight as a die) and the other, that in mediaeval times Rudheath had been a sanctuary for anyone fleeing from justice. If a criminal or person who was thought to have offended against the law could hide out here for a year and a day, they would be free from pursuit and punishment from then on. It is amusing to read Ormerod, the great historian of Cheshire, on this subject in the nineteenth century. He says, "It was observable that the numerous cottages and dwellings around the solitary lanes contain inhabitants whose objectives are not dissimilar from the lawless race who in ancient times were offered protection." So much for our part of the world in those days!

Among the small staff of five teachers was a spinster who was possessed of a short temper and sharp tongue. She would throw a book at your head if the occasion demanded and never suffered fools gladly; we always felt that she thought that she should have been headmistress. There were heated arguments between her and the headmaster as she sought to dominate him. The boys used to be highly amused as they watched the red flush which came over her face and descended down her neck. She really was a terror to children who were not up to standard. Her academic qualities were not to be questioned, but her method of applying these was the stumbling block. On one occasion she gave me twopence and an 'early' mark for reciting poetry without mistakes, which meant that I was allowed out of school five minutes early. Another time, on a hot summer's day when I was sitting in a daydream, she crept up on me and soundly whacked me across my head! I remember to this day what a shock it gave me and how my ears rang. Many an irate parent came to the school to complain about her treatment of their offspring, all to no avail. I well remember one lad receiving a blow from her across his ear with a book, and the boy's mother sending him to school with a note informing the teacher that he had 'bad ears', suffering ear-ache from time to time. Our class had a side door which opened out onto the infants' playground and this is where various angry parents came knocking. Heated arguments were overheard by us in class although we never witnessed what happened for, as a rule, the door was closed.

Another of our teachers was very old fashioned in her outlook and also in her dress; she must have been well into middle-age, with skimpy hair, when she taught me. She had a mannerism of moistening the chalk with her tongue before writing on the blackboard and often there was chalk dust around her lips. I remember her teaching us our multiplication tables by repetition. We would all have to stand and repeat "once two is two", "two twos are four", and so on until it bored into our brains. She was not quite as hard on discipline as the other teacher but she had a nasty habit of clutching one's shoulder in chastisement, pinching the skin between her thumb and finger at the same time, making us cringe and squirm. I came up against her later on when I was about thirteen and she had been directed to teach our class. On this particular day she caught me reading a letter that a boy had sent to me, just a naive and innocent note: she commanded me to stand in front of the class and read it out loud to everyone. I panicked as I stepped out from behind the desk, which I shared with five other children (it being one of the long old-fashioned desks). There was no way I would have read my little note out loud to anyone, let alone all those attentive faces, so, as I passed the open fireplace, I dropped it into the flames. The teacher was furious with me for foiling her, and accused me of being too big for my shoes, which I probably was at that age. The outcome of that little fracas was that I got a hundred, or was it two hundred, lines to write out after school — "I must be obedient".

There was always somebody or other being 'kept in' after school, often for some small misdemeanour. I think it annoyed us more than 'the Stick'.

The teacher I have spoken of had been courting for years and shortly after this episode left to get married. We all brought our pennies to the headmaster and between us managed to raise enough money to buy her a woollen travelling rug to take with her on her honeymoon, to the Canary Islands.

Our other woman teacher was much younger; she wore her hair over her ears in coils known as 'earphones', which were very popular at the time. She was also engaged to be married and her fiancé sometimes rode over on his bicycle to meet her from school. We thought that he was very handsome, as we watched them mount their cycles and ride down the lane. It was quite a distance to her home which was near the locks at Vale Royal. She was a good teacher and much more lenient than the other two women. When punishment was handed out she would invariably remove her engagement ring before slapping a child's legs.

The youngest teacher to be added to our staff was straight from college, and so Welsh that it took us a little while to get used to his manner of speech. His name was David Evans, and once we got to know him we liked him very much. He was especially popular with the boys because he was very good on games and the older boys enjoyed helping him to maintain the school garden once a week. I liked him because of his music lessons, when he taught us 'The Gentle Dove', 'David of the

White Rock', and other Welsh tunes. Our headmaster was also very fond of music and during playtime would often play the piano for his own pleasure. I sometimes crept back into the classroom to listen to him playing 'The Londonderry Air', which he was adamant should be called by its correct name. How I loved to hear it. When I was in his class he often kept us after school if he thought that we had not sung well enough. This made us late and it was therefore a big temptation for us to walk home along the canal, which was close by the school and the quickest way home but was out of bounds. When we took this risk, we would first of all watch the headmaster mount his bicycle and disappear dawn the lane. Then, taking to our heels, we would soon reach home. The peculiar thing was that, although there never seemed to be anyone about at the time, the next morning the teacher would always know what we had been up to. It never failed to get us a whack on our hands from his cane.

The canal featured largely in our lives and during the school holidays we used it often. The only people to use the canal tow-path after school were the teacher with the quick temper and the school caretaker, a wispy little woman with grey hair and a keen sense of humour. She lived in one of the cottages in Broken Cross Place and was very hard working. At Christmas she would bring bags of sweets to school, throwing them among the children who would scrabble after them.

Chapter Six

The canal – shown here in a smoky mist – was a vital artery for trade during the author's childhood. (Photograph courtesy of Cheshire Museums Services)

There was constant traffic, the Trent and Mersey Canal being a busy waterway when we were children. Narrow-boats brought coal from the Midlands and returned loaded with salt. The "boaties" would pull in at the Inn alongside the canal.

*W*e had the freedom to roam the countryside, even when solitary. Children of today do not have this pleasure, for obvious reasons. That is one of the saddest things of our time, that they cannot enjoy the kind of freedom that we revelled in. Toys and money are no substitute for this. We wandered in a leisurely way together in small gangs, sometimes six or seven of us at a time, both boys and girls. Luscious blackberries grew along the canal banks and hedgerows, and 'heathen' berries hung heavy on the hawthorn bushes in autumn. There was always a deposit of grime or dust left around our lips when we had eaten them. When I was a small child, Mother would ask "Have you been eating heathen berries?" on replying "No", I would receive a sharp slap for telling fibs. I never learned. It was the same in Spring when we ate the new green leaves of the hawthorn, calling it 'bread and cheese'.

As we walked along by the canal side we would watch the boys 'skimming' small flat stones over the surface of the water. We would join in but were never quite as good at it as the boys. When we wandered in the meadows there were other things which we chewed and ate with safety, for there were no dangerous sprays used then. We would pick the leaves of 'sour grass', which were comparatively small, placing them together one on another until we had made a thick 'sandwich', which made our mouths water with its acid taste. I believe its proper name is 'Sorrel'. Then there was the flat creamy nut which we extracted from the purple thistle, pricking our fingers as we dissected the flower to get to the nut underneath. Another favourite was the sweet briar picked from the branches in the hedgerows. I suppose the information on what was safe to eat and what was not was handed down from one generation to another.

As we rambled along, the girls picked the wild flowers. There were lovely bluebell woods scattered here and there: Frith's Wood, for instance, later to be chopped out of existence to make way for the Northwich bypass and Parry's Wood, on the way to Whatcroft Hall, happily still there. Apart from the bluebells, we liked to pick 'Ragged Robin' which was the pretty pink Campion, 'Lady's Smocks', the delicate mauve flowers of marshy meadows, dog daisies, the 'White Star of Bethlehem', so fragile that it had always drooped before we reached home, violets, celandines and king-cups (marsh marigolds from the woodland). Picking daisies took up a lot of time for we usually made chains to place around our necks and crowns to put on our heads. one flower we avoided like the plague, the hedge parsley we called 'Mother Die'; obviously we were not going to tempt fate by taking it home among our bouquets.

In the school playing fields, where cricket matches were held in the summer, shaking grass grew abundantly and it was a great pleasure to me to wander down to the bottom of the field and find it there nodding and quaking among the common grass. It's very rarely that I see it nowadays. Dandelions we were loath to pick, for the common name for them was 'pee beds', but we did like to blow the 'clocks' when the flowers had gone to seed — "one o'clock, two o'clock" we would chant, as the tiny seed puffs floated away on the breeze. From time to time you will hear people remarking that summers are not what they used to be and, on reflection, I think that this is true.

During our school summer holidays we would take a bottle of tap water and a few jam 'butties' and set off for 'Dane fields', there to stay for most of the day. There was no need for mackintoshes or any other protection — the weather would be so warm. There was one particular spot for which we usually made a bee-line, this was a wide sandbank where the River Dane cut and wound its way through the meadows. The water was shallow hereabouts, and we could wade across to the other bank but there were one or two 'whirly pools' to beware of. We always knew that the next day was going to be fine and warm, if the evening sky was rosy red. Also, if very early in the morning there was a heavy mist over the meadows, we could rely on the mist melting away leaving the sun to produce yet another hot summer's day. It would seem that nowadays such signs are not to be trusted, for after a heavy mist in the early morning I have known the day to turn out disappointingly wet.

On our carefree travels there was a place that we visited

which will always be associated with tranquillity in my memory. It was known locally as 'Table Mountain' and was a flat-topped hill which overlooked the winding river Dane and the nearby village of Davenham with its lovely church spire soaring upwards. It made a beautiful picture. The larks would rise up from the meadows higher and higher singing in the most heavenly way, while we lay on our backs in the long grass looking up at the blue sky above our heads and hidden from view. We loved to hide like this so that no-one knew where we were; it gave us a secret feeling of power. There was a right of way from the lane across 'Table Mountain' down to the river bank and stile which led into the main road through the village. The entrance is now obscured by overgrown hedges, and I think that few young people know of its existence today.

The canal bridge at Broken Cross which we walked over on one of our chosen routes to school had three huge and beautiful elm trees growing at the foot. All of us, at one time or another, had stretched out our arms to see how far they would go round their massive trunks. They were cut down some years ago when the bridge was strengthened and widened to allow heavy traffic to cross over it. Across the road from the trees were four cottages, which still remain, and a blacksmith's shop. In the large house on the corner lived the wheelwright and his family. The smithy is now obsolete as far as shoeing horses is concerned. It used to be busy looking after both the horses from the farms around and also with the horses which drew the narrow-boats. The 'boaties' as we called them would pull in at the inn alongside the canal which had stables where the horses could be fed and watered, and the bargees themselves would get refreshments. There was constant traffic to and fro, the Trent and Mersey Canal being a busy waterway when we were children. Narrow-boats brought coal from the Midlands and returned loaded with salt. As we eyed up the boats, we would be filled with curiosity to know what the tiny cabins up front were like, and once our curiosity got the better of us. While the occupants were enjoying themselves in the pub one evening, two or three of us dared one another to creep aboard and take a quick peep inside. Afterwards, we were filled with admiration for we had never seen such tiny living quarters, with brasses that literally shone like gold, ornaments brightly painted in reds and greens and two little bunk beds, one above the other. Everywhere was immaculate.

The tow paths are now overgrown with weeds and the only traffic is pleasure boats, their engines put-putting along the canal. A visit to the cottages on the bridge was often on our agenda as we went to school. In summer there was home-brewed dandelion or nettle 'pop' to be had at a halfpenny for a small bottle and a penny for a large one. How we loved its tangy taste on a hot day. In the winter, the same lady who made the 'pop' also made treacle toffee, as did the old lady next door to her. Sometimes it was overcooked but although it tasted harsh we could hardly bring ourselves to throw it away. I have yet to taste anything more vile than burnt treacle toffee! Another port of call was the small shop on the canal bank not far from the inn. This is where the bargees would call for groceries. The bell always jangled loudly as we opened the shop door, calling forth Miss Burgess to see to us at the well scrubbed counter. Crusty new bread stood to one side and, more in our line, bottles of sweets to be hovered over as we held our halfpenny and pennies in our hands. Miss Burgess was a small quietly spoken lady who taught us in Sunday School and was engaged to one of the brothers who helped to run the farm at the bottom of Broken Cross Place. Alas, he died before they could marry.

If we walked to school by way of King Street, the old Roman Road, we passed Canal Side Farm where work went quietly ahead most of the time, except in the autumn when the big threshing machine paid its 'visitation'. There were usually a few boys and girls hanging around on the side-lines watching what went on. I remember the din, above all the throbbing of the engine, the dust that billowed about the farm-yard, and the men energetically filling the sacks with grain as it poured out of the 'Thresher'. Standing next door to the farm and set well back from the road was Gough's Cottage, very old and thatched. Here we got a 'hatful' of small pears for ½d or a 'pinny-full' for a penny.

At the corner of School Lane was our little Church of St Thomas; it is still there but minus its bell (it went during the Second World War) which rang out for us on Sundays. We attended the church on Sunday mornings, went to Sunday School in the afternoon, which was held in our day-school, and often went to church again for Evensong. Certain clothes were put aside for Sunday; it was unthinkable to wear your best on any other day. At this time, while the Council estate was still in its infancy and not extensive as it is today, the head of our parish was Canon Saunders who was a tall, heavily-built gentleman with a deep booming voice, altogether an impressive character. He lived in a beautiful Georgian rectory at Davenham, as we were not in the parish of Witton in those days. Now, a small modern rectory stands next to the old one. He visited his flock from time to time and I well remember him calling on us and my feeling overawed as he sat in Dad's armchair chatting with my parents.

How much slower day-to-day life was in those days — no blaring transistors, not much traffic on the roads, altogether a quieter way of life. I specially recall the consideration extended to people who were seriously ill. Sometimes tree-bark was laid down outside the house of a very sick person to deaden the sound of wheels of a vehicle passing by. I remember creeping past one house with a playmate where a lady lay seriously ill and we whispered to one another, "She's not expected to get better." Nowadays, noise is part of everyday life.

One hot summer evening I had been to church with my cousin and her friends, and, as we emerged from the cool interior of the building, we were looking for something to do for a couple of hours. There had been rumours of an old man living somewhere in the back lanes in a home-made dwelling of sorts, having temporarily left his family to live out in the fields, and on this particular Sunday evening we decided to find out if there was any truth in it. Clambering over a five-barred gate we entered a field and looked for signs of habitation. Finding nothing of interest we wandered off into another field, and then another. Suddenly, someone's sharp eyes detected something in the distance that spurred us on. As we approached the object of our attention, we realised that it was a small wooden shack which had been built over a deep dry ditch, the roof held firm with lumps of turf. Three of us kept 'nicks' (look-out) while the bravest one crept nearer to make sure that the little shack was unoccupied. We listened and waited for a while, then plucked up courage and followed our leader. No need to have worried; all was quiet and there was not a soul about. We opened the door of the little lean-to and as our eyes got accustomed to the poor light within, a pleasant sight revealed itself to us. The sides of the shack had been papered to give the illusion of a comfortable little home, and a bunk bed filled one end of it. An alarm clock was ticking away on a shelf above the bed, and, for some reason, this seemed to make everything more exciting. One last, quick glance showed us a small chamber pot underneath the bunk-bed.

There was no more time to loiter for the look-out had imagined that she had seen some movement in the distance and we prepared to flee. Nothing happened, however, and we sauntered away from the place, giggling and discussing our discovery. Suddenly, our peace was shattered as we heard an angry voice hailing us. The farmer had crept up on us unawares, shaking his stick aloft menacingly. He began to chase us, at the same time setting his large black collie dog on us. That was the last straw as far as I was concerned, as I had a great fear of dogs. I took to my heels, my feet hardly touching the ground. The other three followed breathlessly until I fell headlong over a large tuft of grass just as I was within reach of the gate. We glanced wildly around, too tired to move another step but, thankfully, the farmer had called the dog off and was making off in another direction. We fell about laughing with hysteria and relief. The funniest thing about this was that I had my knee bandaged and in fact I had been limping for a few days, not being able to bend it. It was sore but, in my fright, I never felt its pain or even remembered it.

The church bell was rung on Sundays by a youth who suffered from epilepsy. On no account could he be induced to let anyone else perform this task unless he was ill. I had a cousin who was an epileptic, a quiet, clever lad. Most Sundays, if we went up into the little balcony of the church, there he would be, standing under the low roof of the building, ringing the bell and guarding the bell rope for dear life in case we should ask to have a go.

I visited the Parish churchyard once with a cousin to try to locate our great grandparents' grave. We had heard it described among our relatives on many occasions, so off we went to find it. We did, and as we stood there reading the names of our forebears, felt quite satisfied with ourselves. Before returning home, my cousin's eyes alighted on the rubbish heap which stood next to several tall, dark holly trees. There, on top of the heap, were recently discarded flowers from someone's grave. She pounced on them to take home to her mother, for they still appeared quite fresh. On arriving at my aunt's house, my cousin handed over the flowers, saying, "I've bought these for you, Mam!" My aunt examined the bright, expensive flowers and fixed my cousin with a steely eye, enquiring where she had got them from. Under her mother's stern gaze, she was forced to admit that they were from the cemetery. Sparks flew, and so did I, as my aunt threatened what she would do if she ever did such a thing again and flung the flowers out of the house.

When the Council estate was still comparatively newly built, not long after the First World War, we often had ex-servicemen singing in the street, and holding out a cap to receive the coppers which came their way. Their service medals were pinned across their chests and they leaned on a crutch if they had been maimed during the war. Sometimes a man would possess a good voice, while others would leave a lot to be desired but, regardless of this, we couldn't wait to rush out and place a coin into the cap held in an outstretched hand. It was a sad sight. At one time there was a Scottish soldier, complete with kilt and regalia, who played his bagpipes as he marched smartly up and down the road. He would gather quite a crowd of children who, after watching his performance for a short while, fell in behind and imitated his actions, turning when he turned, until he became exasperated and shooed them all away.

A knife grinder used to come around crying "scissors to grind, knives to grind", and often we had a man selling props, shouting "clothes' props, line props". As the days grew shorter and darkness came early, the children would gather in small groups after tea to have one last fling before bedtime. Inevitably, we would gravitate towards the newly erected shed which was our grocer's shop. There was another building identical to this one in the next avenue, but somehow the shop in our road was where we all accumulated. Everybody liked the shopkeeper, and later on his fiancée, whom he introduced to our parents. We loved the brightness which exuded from this small building and would stare in at the window playing 'I spy' and other guessing games. In general we larked about until our parents called us home to bed.

Dad knew Billy, the shopkeeper, for they had both served with the 'Cheshires' in the First World War and had volunteered for service while still only in their teens. Sometimes I accompanied Dad when he went to buy his fags, twopenny packets of Woodbines, but when the two got started on their memories of war escapades there was no stopping them. I would then become fidgety and when Billy realised that I was still around, he would bring me one or two tiny star-like biscuits that had a bit of icing on the top and I would skip off home. No doubt that was the reason why I accompanied Dad in the first place! Billy was a small curly-haired fellow and had a scar on his forehead. He said that it had been caused when, as a prisoner of war, a German had attacked him with a heavy piece of oak. As the years went by and the population grew, more houses were built and the shed disappeared, to be replaced by a good solid house and shop. Then a sub post office was installed as the business prospered.

When the population was relatively small everyone knew everyone else, and on summer evenings there were always one or two people to be seen chatting together at their gates, sometimes until quite late. We played lots of games in the avenues and as each season came around so the games would change accordingly. If it was skipping time most of the road was taken up by a rope stretched across it, held by a girl at each end. Nobody wanted this job, they much preferred to show off their ability to skip and do various twists and turns in the rope.

Often we borrowed our mother's clothes' lines to play with. Then there was 'trundle' time, when our wooden hoops would be bowled along and kept going as long as possible by being tapped with a small stick. Top and whip was another great favourite; the whip often a bit of a stick with string attached and the tops brightly coloured with chalks or bits of silver paper. We played hop-scotch and games where we marched around in circles chanting songs such as 'The Farmer Takes a Wife', then there was 'Oranges and Lemons' which ended with a tug o' war — all this activity going on in the middle of the road. We were disturbed very little by traffic in those days.

We played marbles and 'Jacks' or five stones, playing at marbles on the earth playground at school and 'Jacks' on the stone-flagged floor of the girls' cloakroom. My mother made me many a small 'Dorothy bag', from bits of remnants or patchworks, in which to carry my marbles but, as quickly as I bought a ha'porth they would be won from me. This always annoyed me secretly as I saw my nice new store disappear into someone else's bag. It was worse still if they were my glass alleys with their lovely coloured stripes for they were slightly more expensive.

The butcher, baker and Co-op brought their goods to us by horse and cart. It was a common sight to see a child shovelling up the manure which the horses had left behind, for the father to spread around his roses in the garden. They seem to thrive on the heavy clay soil hereabouts. In the dry hot summers a watering cart came around the neighbourhood sprinkling water over the dusty roads as it passed by, like a great watering can. Once, I remember, when there was a drought, we went to collect buckets of water from the pump in the yard of the old white cottage that stood in a large garden next to the St John's Infant School. It has since been demolished and replaced by a car park.

Mother used to make us a tasty confection which she called Chester Cake. The tin would be lined with pastry and filled with a mixture of soaked breadcrumbs, egg, sugar and currants, if I remember rightly, and it was delicious. As I walked to school one day when I was quite young I was joined by a lad who lived a few doors away who, for some reason, was carrying a tiny copper kettle in his hand. I have always been attracted by tiny miniature objects and asked him if I could carry it for a while. His answer was "only if you give me a bit of your cake". Loath though I was to part with it, the miniature kettle won; he had the last piece of my cake, and I carried the kettle all the way to school.

Although we didn't live far from school, when it was very cold in winter we stayed for dinners. I still have the small basket in which I carried my food. It was an exact replica of one Dad took to work. In it went the little meat pies that were homemade and sometimes, as a change, bacon butties. Those who stayed in dinners sat facing the headmaster at his table. He would often bring hard boiled eggs for his meal, tapping them on his plate and carefully stripping off the shells. There was no set regime for our dinners, we just stayed or went home as we pleased.

As a rule, my sister and I went to bed early on dark nights and, although I usually went to sleep as soon as my head touched the pillow, there was the odd occasion when I didn't drop off so easily. If everyone was quiet and I couldn't hear my mother moving about downstairs, I would shout "Are you there, Mam?" and her reassuring voice would come back to me, "Of course I'm here," as she darned our socks or did some such chore. A little later I would hear the gramophone being played next door. Often it would be a Sousa march, which would remind me of my grandparents, and listening to the music drifting faintly through the walls I would soon be lulled off to sleep.

Chapter Seven

Witton Brook following the collapse of Platts Hill Rock Salt Mine in December 1880. (Photograph courtesy of Cheshire County Council Libraries and Archives).

In Winter the sheets of water which were numerous in our area would be frozen over. The larger stretches originated from the indiscriminate pumping of brine which caused the land to cave in.

In Winter the sheets of water which were numerous in our area would be frozen over. (The Winters seemed much colder when I was a child and the Summers hotter.) Many of these ponds, or pits as we called them, were the result of people many years ago digging for marl, a bluey-grey clay. Gradually, these large round pits filled with rain-water and, as nature took over, reeds and many lovely wild flowers grew round the edges. Today, I think that they are an attractive feature of our Cheshire countryside, though there aren't as many as there were owing to building and development. There are larger stretches of water too, originating from the pumping of brine when it was allowed to be pumped indiscriminately. This caused the land to cave in and collapse in various parts of the district. We called these larger pits 'flashes', but it was to the smaller ponds that we resorted when they were frozen over.

How we delighted in this sliding back and forth on the thick ice, kept warm as toast by all our activity. We couldn't wait to get out of school. Just one thing marred our happiness and that was the constant wearing through of our shoe soles. Nevertheless, although Dad threatened to replace my shoes with wooden clogs that had steel tips, I could never keep away from the ice for long. I remember a lad of thirteen almost as tall as his father, who used to come 'skating' with our gang, until, one day, he looked up to see his father approaching and taking off his leather belt as he drew nearer. The lad was gone like a shot, his father after him. It must have been a constant headache for our parents to keep us in shoe leather when their warnings went unheeded.

The deepest pit on which we played, unlike the others, had sloping sides which we had to clamber down to get on the ice. It was situated in a large piece of open ground which was known as the Common, close to a ruined old factory. Here, during the first World War, TNT had been manufactured. This dark reddish powder was an explosive used in the firing of shells. I believe that some of this horrible stuff had been dumped in the deep pit which we skated on after the war had ended. Certainly I remember that the bare soil had a dark red tinge to it which was not to be seen elsewhere. It makes me shiver to contemplate what would have happened if the ice had cracked. Alongside the ruins of the factory was a narrow-gauge railway line, with platforms and so on, and this also became our playground.

We were playing in the Avenues one evening when word went around that large fires were burning in a farm field in Penny's Lane; I believe it was Caldwell's Farm. A gang of us set off over Broken Cross Bridge to investigate. Tall thick hedges full of thorns divided us from the field but, as we stood by the roadside, the huge bonfires which had been lit were reaching up into the sky and illuminating all around. As we peered between the hedges, we could see cattle being led from the farmyard to where large pits had been dug, men passing to and fro in front of the fires and cattle falling to the ground. It was like a scene from Dante's 'Inferno' and, as dusk increased and night fell, we all hurried back home over the canal bridge. This scene, where a farm had been visited by Foot and Mouth Disease, has stayed vividly in my mind all these years.

Although electricity was laid on for us by the Mid-Cheshire Electric Light Company, in the beginning it was solely for lighting up our homes. My mother says that the charge was one and fourpence a week however much was used and that some families kept their lights on all through the night. It's not surprising that the system was altered after a while and the charge raised. Later still, each household was supplied with a grill-cum-boiling plate, with which came an attractive square-based copper kettle. During the General Strike in 1926, we still needed coal for warmth and cooking and as our stock of coal dwindled our parents had to think of other ways of supplementing it. There had already been a hive of industry around the old gas works in the town with people buying bags of coke and trundling it away on small trucks, old prams, bikes and what-have you. We found a temporary solution by joining neighbours who were picking cinders from the railway embankment about a mile away from our house. 'Needs must when the devil drives!' It was a quiet track where the engine seemed to creep stealthily up on us as it rounded the bend so we had to keep a sharp look-out. The second time that we went on this expedition (and our last) a fireman from a passing train threw out some large lumps of coal for us and waved as the engine picked up speed and vanished into the distance. The few precious spoils were divided between us and there was a great feeling of friendliness and comradeship as we made for home, for we were all in the same boat. I remember there was a large pond in a field next to this embankment, with bushes and reeds around its edge, where we occasionally saw a kingfisher flashing by and also where we would watch 'Billybriz', our nickname for dragonflies, hover and skim over the water in Summer.

I joined the Brownies with three other girls from Rudheath, walking a couple of miles to the 'Neuman Room' where our meetings were held once a week. It was next to Witton Parish Church and all was well when I had the companionship of the other girls, but I remember once that I had to go on my own and that was a different state of affairs as the last bit of the journey led down Church Walk steps and past the churchyard. It was surrounded by a low stone wall so, consequently, I could just see the tops of the gravestones in the gathering darkness. I took to my heels and ran breathlessly the rest of the way. I enjoyed going and kept up a fairly good attendance over a period of about two years. Later I joined the Girl Guides and eventually we went camping with them near Barmouth in Wales. We filled large sacks with straw from the farm nearby for our beds, bought butter and eggs from the farmer and soon made ourselves at home. I even relished the smoky porridge (I had always refused to eat porridge at home!) and the bacon, which tasted similar, that we cooked over the camp fire. It was an exhilarating experience, bathing early in the morning in the swift-running River Wynnion, icy cold from the mountains. The biggest thrill of all was climbing Cader Idris with our Welsh guide. As we stood with him near the summit, we kept still and close together as he had told us to do while the mountain mist which had descended upon us swirled around. We couldn't see a hand before us and then the mist lifted, disappearing as quickly as it had come, to reveal a wonderful view of the valley down below. It was the first time that I had been away on my own and I have always remembered the pleasure it gave me.

When a new boy was seen in our Avenue it didn't take long for us to spot him for we all knew one another. Inevitably, the two of us met and soon found out that our mothers had lived next door to one another as children. It was pleasant for his mother and mine to recall old times together and soon we became friends. I remember reading the large encyclopaedias, edited by Arthur Mee, which stood in the front room of his parents' house, and believe that my interest in art was sparked off by looking at the pictures painted by famous artists and reading about their lives. In contrast to this interest in books, tree-climbing was high on our agenda, for I was a real tom-boy and the more difficult a tree the better I liked it. There were plenty to choose from in those days, though they have all now gone from this part of the estate.

The cuckoo visited us bang on time in early Spring, and from then on his plaintive call could be heard for the rest of the Spring and Summer until his voice became croaked and muffled and he was ready to fly away. As the oaks and hedgerows have disappeared, so has he.

Jumping ditches was another of our favourite pastimes and there were several around the perimeter of the meadows encircling our homes. These ditches ran with clear water and watercress would often be growing in them, with Ladys' Smocks growing along the banks. My young sister, Edith, would follow me, trying to imitate my antics. If I didn't watch her carefully, she would tear her frock or get her feet soaking wet and, on reaching home, we would both be for it. Most of these meadows went as more houses were built on them.

There were plenty of oak leaves to hand when 'Royal Oak Day' came around on 29th May. It was woe-betide anyone who failed to carry a bunch to school. The punishment was a sharp slap around the legs with a bunch of stinging nettles and there was always a 'sharp-shins' lurking around to do just that. I must admit that we loved to catch one another out but the craftiest among us would usually know where the large dock leaves grew, and plucking these would put them on our nettled legs which helped to take away the sting. I don't know if this tradition of remembering King Charles's exploits when he hid in an oak tree from his enemies was local or whether it was played out in other parts of the country.

I never see boys making 'flop guns' nowadays. It was a great pastime for lads when we were young. They made them from hollowed out pieces of 'Ella' (elderberry wood), using acorns for ammunition. They could be lethal if used carelessly and, like their home-made catapults, were confiscated by the teachers if they took them to school. The boys played a game which they called 'peggy'. Fashioning a short stick out of a thick piece of wood and tapering it at both ends, they would place it on the ground and hit one end of it with a stick causing it to fly into the air. While it was airborne, they would see how far they could strike it and the one who sent the 'peggy' the farthest was the winner. On the first day of April, Fools' Day, we played the usual practical jokes on one another until twelve o'clock mid-day, then it was all change to 'legging down time'. We would catch hold of someone's legs, pulling them down on the ground if we could. I have never found out where this game originated.

Nowadays, children have so many possessions that to them our way of life may seem to have been humdrum or even boring. We rarely travelled far afield or had expensive toys, yet it took very little to make us happy.

Boring was a word we never used in our childhood days. Our imagination came into play to make up for the lack of material things and, most of all, we had freedom to wander at will in the countryside. There were, of course, those things we would dearly have loved to have had. For instance, I was obsessed at one time with bicycles. Few of my schoolmates had one but we usually managed to cadge a ride from the lucky ones who did. I did a 'swap' with my wooden scooter one day for a ride on a girl's bicycle! Although I was able to mount the machine while someone held it steady and ride down the Avenue, I soon realised that I didn't know how to pull up and dismount, not having been on a bicycle before, so I pedalled along until I fell off.

Another obsession I had was for a piano but it would have been useless for me to have pestered for one. "I can't knock blood out of a stone," Mother would have said. So I did the next best thing and accompanied a girl who studied music when she went for her lessons. Her music teacher was quite affable about this and allowed me to sit on a chair while she put my friend through her paces. Whenever I hear 'Robins Return' being played it conjures up a picture for me of this girl, her fingers moving nimbly over the piano keys. She was not too clever with her school work but she played the piano beautifully and gained her cap and gown when she was older. The other girl who lived in my immediate area and whose parents owned a piano, was also one of my classmates. I liked her very much and would call for her as I passed by on my way to school. She had jobs to do before going to school, because her mother was not in the best of health, and we would often find ourselves running breathlessly all the way, as arriving late could mean 'the stick' for us. When her parents were out, I would call on her, ostensibly to play but always in the back of my mind was the intention to have a go on the piano. I don't remember any of the rest of the family being interested in playing it themselves but my friend and her elder sister were very patient in the way that they put up with my constant attempts to play the 'Londonderry Air' with one finger.

Life did get a bit monotonous at times, but it wouldn't be long before something 'cropped up'. Something did one day, as a group of us lingered on the bridge looking down on the canal on our way home from school. We saw something moving slowly towards us in the water. As it drew closer we realised, with a shiver of excitement, that it was a white horse still fastened by its rope to the narrow-boat it had been towing, and which was still sailing gently along behind it. Evidently the poor animal had plodded too near to the canal's edge at some stage of its journey and fallen into the water. It was not unknown to us that some of these boat-horses got weary and were prone to accidents but we had never seen such a thing before. As it neared the bridge, the bargee walked alongside accompanied by a man from another boat which had come up from round the bend. They had thrown a rope over the horse's head to keep it under control, thus preventing it from getting into the middle of the canal. It looked like something out of a fairy story, this white horse prancing up and down casting spray in all directions as its hooves dipped into the water and came up again. By now, nothing would have deterred us from seeing this to a conclusion so we ran down to the towpath, walking on ahead of the 'procession'. The men had two attempts at trying to haul the poor beast out of the water but on each occasion its hooves failed to get a hold on the slippery sandstone and it slid back again looking very scared. At last we were almost at the inn by the next bridge when the 'procession' halted at a large iron ring attached to some boards on the canal bank. We had often seen it but were quite unprepared for what happened next. One of the men bent dawn and tugged on the iron ring and, lo and behold, it came up off the ground like a huge heavy lid on a box, revealing some shallow stone steps leading down into the canal. The horse was manoeuvred into position, the men pulled on the rope, and, with a clatter of iron-shod hooves, it just walked up out of the water. With a sigh of relief, we watched it being freed of its harness and, after it had rested for a very short time (I suppose the bargees had got behind with their schedule), it was harnessed up to the boat again. The man in charge whipped the horse and it began to run, with him shouting all the while as boat and horse disappeared under the canal bridge and into the distance. We had felt so worried for the horse in its predicament that this was the last straw, and we shouted after the man and called him cruel. Someone standing around said that it was being treated in that manner so that it wouldn't catch pneumonia!

There was another occasion when a boat-horse had had an accident and died at the stables which were once part of the Broken Cross Inn. When we arrived on the scene, some men were covering it up with sack-bags as it lay on its side on an open cart. As it was being driven off to the knacker's yard up the steep incline to the road, some of the bags were dislodged as the poor animal's stiff legs jogged up and down with the swaying of the cart. We felt quite sad as we watched it go.

Chapter Eight

Cranage Mill, site of the heroic rescue described earlier and a favourite place for excursions by local people. (Photograph courtesy of Pauline Bradbury)

At harvest time we would go into the fields to "help" gather in the hay. We would pester the farm labourers to let us have a go at using a pickel and if this was refused we would chase each other round till the hay-cart was piled high and making a return journey to the farmyard.

When I was capable of travelling further afield on my own, I walked along the canal bank to visit my grandparents. Time was saved by going that way instead of by Griffith's Road. When I left the canal bank my path lay over a piece of waste ground which was divided from the chemical works by high black boards and where weeds and grasses grew tall. Cinder-flowers (Rose bay willow herbs) grew there in pinky-mauve masses but, although I felt tempted to pick a bunch of the lovely flowers, I knew from past experience that they would have wilted before my journey's end. After a short while I would reach the railway arch, calling "cuckoo" as I always did so that I could hear the echo as I passed underneath it. With not far to go, I would be pleasantly anticipating the tit-bits, such as pork crackling, that Granny would have ready for me. Alice, my young aunt, was living at home with my grandparents, but married now to Arthur and with a small child of her own.

The time always went by very quickly and soon it seemed I was getting ready to return home. To make sure that I didn't return the way I had come, Granny always asked Alice to accompany me as far as the canal bridge. This she did willingly and, after warning me not to go off with anyone, would wait until I was well on my way up the road. I rarely saw anyone except the narrow-boat people, but one thing did bother me and that was the fear of meeting a horse at a spot where boards ran alongside the canal bank. This made the path more narrow and hemmed in so that if I did meet one it inevitably looked as though it was making a beeline for me as it plodded along. I would try to make myself as small as possible, cringing hard up against the boards until it had gone by.

In the summer we had our Sunday School treat to look forward to. It was a boat trip on the canal to Whatcroft Hall, a country house a few miles from Rudheath. Dear old canal, what would we have done without you? It was responsible for some tragic drownings and even several suicides over the years, but we, as small children, had not a care in the world as we boarded our brightly painted narrow-boat beside the Inn, raring to go on our annual trip. All dressed up in our Sunday best clothes, we were as thrilled as if we were embarking on a long cruise. With a "gee-up" the horse would move on, pulling the rope taut as it drew us and the boat behind it.

What a pleasant way of travelling it was!

In just half an hour we would be at our destination, all too soon for we enjoyed sailing along on the water. But there would be more enjoyment to come as we followed one another in a crocodile up the embankment and into the parkland surrounding the 'big house', where our benefactors awaited us.

After a greeting, we were allowed to go and play as we wished, on the long swing hanging from a huge oak tree's branches, racing one another, or playing other games until tea was set out for us on a long trestle table in the shade of some willows beside the lake. It was always said that if it rained we would be allowed to have our tea indoors and, on one special occasion, it happened. Most of us had wanted to see inside the Hall, for children are usually inquisitive. We were marched quietly into the house and, as we passed, one of the footmen waiting at the door noticed that a lad had forgotten to remove his cap in his excitement. It was removed for him, swiftly and neatly, as he passed by, never looking to right or left, which looked quite comical as we came up from behind. After gaining access to the Hall, we didn't dare gaze around too freely, showing bad manners, but I remember how lovely the dining room looked as we entered, with its dark polished furniture and flowers. I often wonder what the footmen in their dark blue livery, the brass buttons shining on their striped waistcoats, thought as they waited on all 'us kids' seated at the beautiful long dining table.

After tea, the weather had cleared up and the sun shone so we had had the best of both worlds. Our benefactors had two daughters, Elizabeth and Diana, and as we played they would go riding in the park on their horses and we would say how like princesses they looked. There was one special game that the boys liked best of all. A large wooden roller was set up between two posts and, perched astride this apparatus, two boys holding a pillow each would bash one another until one fell off. How they enjoyed it as we egged them on with our shouts!

As evening drew near, the time came for us to go and we returned to the canal side where our transport was ready and waiting. Mr and Mrs Baerline stood on the bridge with a large basket of oranges to give us one each and to say 'Good-bye'. On two separate occasions, the lady from the Hall visited our school to award me diplomas for essays that I had written; one was on 'hygiene', the other subject escapes me for the moment. I was eleven or so at the time and she might have been awarding me a medal, I was so pleased.

On our way home we usually became a bit rowdy, full of high spirits, and one or two timid girls would seek refuge inside the small cabin as the boys tried to rock the boat. They were sure they would end up in the canal. Miss Burgess, our Sunday School teacher, always calm and in command, would soon put a stop to this nonsense and shortly the old Inn would hove into sight and we would be at our journey's end. Several mothers with small children would be waiting for our arrival, mine among them, and the canal bank would soon be deserted as we made our way home.

You could always tell when there was a special event coming up, for Mother's fingers would be quite pin-pricked at the tips. She used to buy remnants of material from the market and make them up into dresses for my sister and me. They were never very fancy, for dressmaking was not one of her best achievements, but they always turned out quite attractive in the end. There we would be, dressed in identical frocks, alike as two peas in a pod.

The Whit-Sunday walk always started about a mile from our small church, at a farm whose drive was between the Co-op and a row of cottages known as 'Nine Houses', where many a large family was brought up. I remember the lovely golden laburnum trees, the chains of flowers protecting us from the hot sun as we were sorted out into a long procession, each one of us holding gillivers and other flowers picked from the garden. Some had large bouquets, others more insignificant bunches, depending on the kind of garden their parents had. Eventually, we would set out, banners held aloft at the front, walking along the main road until we came to the Avenues, where we detoured and people came out to watch us. After circling the council estate, we would cross the canal bridge and on to our destination, a field opposite the church. Here the crowds gathered for an open air service to be conducted by the Canon and our local clergyman. It was always a very pleasant event with children, parents and officials joining in the hymn-singing with gusto, and nice to be at an open air service for a change instead of inside the church.

As ours was a Church of England school, we had a diversion from the usual lessons once a year, when a reverend gentleman named Mr Pitt visited us. A tall, craggy-faced person, dressed in a black suit and wearing his dog-collar, he would put us through our paces, questioning us on our knowledge of the Bible. He would give twopence to the child who answered the most questions correctly. The school would close at midday after we had all stood up and sung 'Be present ta ta table Lord', for that was how it sounded, and off we would run home to our dinners, happy that we had been granted the afternoon off.

Washing day did indeed last nearly all day. On dark mornings, Mother would be up before cock-crow to start on the laundry, dolly tub and dolly peg at the ready. The iron boiler stood in one corner of the bathroom, which was downstairs, with the bath itself being fitted along one wall. There was not a lot of room between it and the boiler. This was very nice and comfortable for us if we were having a bath on a cold night, a fire being lit in the small grate underneath the boiler to heat the water. Of course, in hot weather it would become too much of a good thing. To avoid using the electric light early on, Mother lit a candle and by its light scrubbed the clothes on the long wooden lid which covered the bath when it was not in use. She then boiled the calico sheets and pillow slips in the boiler and anything else which she considered necessary. She was a great believer in treating the laundry in this way and, in consequence, many a thing became faded prematurely. Most people did the same thing and in fact one woman who lived near us always insisted on boiling her white lace curtains on wash days.

Dyeing was very popular around this time, as was calico. If the cheaper unbleached type was bought it could be boiled until it became as snow white as the bleached material and was harder wearing. Used as bed linen, it was very economical and, dyed to one's choice of colour, it made good curtains. Lots of furnishings around the house were dyed to give more colour because the fashion for doors and window-frames was a drab dark brown, with the walls often painted a dark green.

I remember the electric light fittings being made of brass and how, on one occasion, as my mother switched the light on in the bathroom, she received a shock up her arm which was, thankfully, not as severe as it might have been. Thereafter, it was switched down with her wooden boiler stick until the matter was put right! We didn't have fittings other than brass for many years, until the coming of bakelite.

Mother got through no end of brushes and soap with all the scrubbing that went on. She wore what she liked to call her 'rough apron' for wash-days, fashioned out of sacking and protecting her from too much of a wetting. 'Perfection', 'Sunlight', and 'Carbolic' soaps were very popular at this time, and Mother swore by 'Carbosil' soap powder for boiling clothes. 'Dolly blue' bags made by Reckitts were used in the rinsing water to whiten clothes, and something called 'Monkey' brand, I think that is the correct name for it — a substance compressed into a hard brown square — was used when damp to clean grease and dirt from the sink and the bath. On looking back, one can appreciate the drudgery involved in keeping a house clean in those days.

There was a 'gentleman farmer' living in the district who served on the local council. Tall and stout, he was usually to be seen dressed in a check jacket, yellow waistcoat, fawn-coloured breeches and leggings, and highly polished brown boots. He was fond of a cigar and more often than not would be smoking one, and I believe that he was fond of a glass of whisky, too. In one way and another he was a good benefactor to the village, and Wrights Avenue and Grange Road are named after him and his farm, perpetuating his memory as far as my generation is concerned. In harvest time we would go into his fields to 'help' gather in the hay. I say this with tongue in cheek, for we must have been more of a hindrance than anything else as we rolled about in the hay.

We would pester the farm labourers to let us have a go at using a pickel so that we could fork up the hay and if this request was refused we would play at 'tick', chasing one another around until the hay-cart was piled high and making a return journey to the farmyard. If we were lucky we got a ride on top of the hay.

There had been talk in the village for some time of a dancing troupe and eventually two ladies joined forces to organise one. We had a well-organised fête founded by members of the Liberal Party and, later, a 'Hospital Saturday' which became an annual event, so, with these in mind, we were launched on our dancing career. One of the ladies was easier to get along with than the other, but if we were to become a successful dance team we had to put up with the discipline, which was only right and proper. Once more our friend the farmer came forward to help us, letting us have the use of his farmyard for our practising for two nights a week. The yard was composed of cobblestones, which was rather hard on our plimsolls, not to mention our feet! An old gramophone was brought along to provide the music, with someone standing by to put on the record and wind up the machine from time to time. If my memory serves me correctly, we danced to the tune of 'A bouquet of roses', a pretty little song which was just right for us, seeing that we were to become the 'Garland Dancers'.

The scene has changed totally since those days. The row of huge elm trees which stood across the lane from the back entrance to the farm have gone long ago, as has the old white house, the little farm cottages further along the lane, and the tiny thatched cottage in its lovely garden opposite to them. I can see them all in my mind's eye with great clarity and, for some strange reason, they seem more real to me than the large modern bakery which has replaced all but the farm.

Fêtes were taken very seriously as far as dancing competitions were concerned, some dancing troupes being quite exotic, and a tremendous amount of work must have gone into the making of some of the costumes. I remember one troupe from Altrincham in particular, who filled us with admiration, if not envy, as we watched them perform, dressed as they were in brilliantly coloured costumes and feathered head-dresses similar to those worn in the film musical 'Rose Marie'. Of course we didn't stand a chance if they were taking part but, because they were older, they were usually in another section which didn't apply to us.

The crowds of spectators that attended these 'do's' would applaud with great enthusiasm as their routine progressed and one of the dancers lit a fire for the Indian braves to caper around. Quite a realistic impression of a fire was created as a firework embedded among the bits of wood was lit and flames and smoke filled the air for a few seconds. This 'Red Indian' spectacle never failed to delight us. Our dance routine was much simpler and our dresses less extravagant. The steps performed were similar to a Morris dance and our dresses were plain white ones with paper roses stitched on here and there. A wreath of paper roses encircled our heads and we held up wooden hoops covered in paper flowers. The end result was quite effective and we all looked rather pretty decked out in our paper roses.

Two or three weeks before entering our first competition there was great activity between one another's homes. Our mothers bought rolls of crêpe paper, which cost very little in those days, and we helped one another to cut up the small squares to be made into rose petals. There was a knack in making paper roses which we acquired with experience and eventually became quite good at. The flowers which we wore around our heads were stitched onto a piece of elastic and, looking at an old photo recently, the thought occurred to me that I could have done with a few more roses attached to my piece of elastic!

We won a silver Charity Shield the first time that we competed, and one or two prizes on other occasions, but as we grew older our troupe underwent a metamorphosis and we became Morris dancers, complete with jingling bells and ruffles, instead of 'Garland Dancers' as we had previously been.

We must have marched for miles at various fêtes in very hot weather and sometimes the tarmac on the roads melted in the brilliant sunshine and stuck to our 'goloshers' as we followed the band. There were one or two good jazz bands in the town and there was much rivalry between the young men as they became more proficient at playing their home-made instruments. 'Yorky Bill', as he was known, was the leader of one band. He was small in stature but very smart and well organised when it came to leading his lads in a competition. These fêtes were a great attraction and created much interest and sociability in the summer months.

Chapter Nine

Dad worked shifts at the chemical works at Lostock. It was originally Bowman Thompsons, was later Brunner Mond and then ICI. In the foreground is Thompsons brick and tile works. (Photograph courtesy of Cheshire County Council Libraries and Archives)

My parents were better off now and we felt the benefit in lots of ways, including having a holiday. Our Mecca was New Brighton and when we reached Liverpool I got the feeling we were living life to the full.

My mother didn't have much to fear regarding our health as children, apart from the fact that my young sister was prone to catching a bronchial cold during the winter. Mother had a remedy for this (when did she not have a remedy for something or other?) and, although it raises a smile now, it did seem to work. As soon as my sister showed signs of a cold settling on her chest, Mother would get a large piece of brown paper, fold it over and cut a hole in the centre large enough to go over her head, trimming the rest of it so that it fitted neatly over her back and chest. Once the 'pattern' had been cut out, it was pricked all over with a needle and, while it was lying flat on the table, it would be rubbed lightly with camphorated oil and sprinkled with a bit of powdered nutmeg. Then, over the child's head it would go, to stay next to her skin night and day until Mother decided that it had 'loosened' her chest and could be removed. What a picture this conjures up, but it did seem to work!

Most people were loathe to send for a doctor unless he was needed urgently and for a very good reason. If you were unlucky enough to require his attention in your own home, you had to pay him in cash when his bill was received. Many working class people were not in a position to do this, so it was a case of paying what you could afford to a 'club-man', who called every week on the doctor's behalf until the bill was settled. The least you were allowed to pay I think was sixpence. So it is understandable why doctors were only called in when absolutely necessary by the majority of folk.

Granny passed on many an old-fashioned remedy to us and one especially used for pains in the stomach was the 'salt bag'. Living so close to where salt was being manufactured from the brine, fine Cheshire salt was always taken for granted in this area. Granny would sew up a piece of material to make a bag, put the coarse salt inside, stitch up the end and then leave it on a warm shelf inside the oven until it was required. She had another remedy for her chest trouble which was aggravated by the fumes and smoke from the salt works and factory chimneys — no smokeless zones then. She would make a linseed poultice for herself by mixing some linseed meal with boiling water so that it became a thick soft paste which was then spread between two pieces of cloth. When it was still very warm she would retire to her bed and place the poultice across her chest. Granny swore by this remedy above all others for relief from her attacks of bronchitis.

When one of my uncles, still living at home and a bachelor, injured his knee badly while playing football, the doctor was called in to give treatment. As time passed and there was no improvement, some 'Job's comforter' murmured "look well if he has to have his leg off!" Grandad came back as usual with a ready retort, saying: "He was born with his leg on and he'll die with his leg on." So saying, he set off to look for some herbs which grew abundantly on waste ground not far from home — 'St. John's Wort' or 'Ragwort', I think, yellow daisy-like flowers on tall stems. Anyway, he gathered them and boiled the flowers and leaves, and bathed Uncle Henry's bad leg, eventually tying the leaves in place around it. This was repeated several times and seemed to do the trick. Uncle Henry lived to be ninety years of age, still in possession of two good legs!

Comfrey was another plant which was used in treatment of conditions like sprains and there were numerous other remedies I am sure which I cannot now recall, except for 'Dolly Blue'. This small bag of blue colouring was, I mentioned before, used in rinsing water to whiten table cloths and linen, but was also used if anyone was unlucky enough to be stung by a bee. I remember being stung as a small child as I sat on a three-legged stool in someone's yard waiting for a friend to come out and play. I felt this horrible pain on my ear and wondered for a split second what had hit me, until the bee buzzed past my face. I remember hurrying home to Granny clutching my ear, but she soon put matters right by dampening the little bag and dabbing it on the painful spot. The pain was soon gone.

Rosie was my best friend. Both twelve years old, we were inseparable at school. She had two grown-up sisters and a brother and, being the youngest, was more protected than the rest of us. Sometimes, of a Summer evening, I went to play with her at Lostock Green. The lane I walked down to get to her house had 'scribble' larks' nests in its banks. The tiny eggs appeared exactly as though a child had doodled on their shells with a pencil and they fascinated me. When I bent down to look at them closely, the air was full of the heavy scent of meadow-sweet, for it grew thickly alongside the hedgerows and ditches with its creamy blossoms. A row of houses now stands in Cooke's Lane, which were not there when I was a schoolgirl.

There are two occasions I recall when we went to the local brine baths. I can't remember why we were allowed to go there on our own, but we did. Rosie had a pair of waterwings which I had a 'go' with. All went well on the first occasion but on the second, while Rosie was splashing about with her waterwings, I was in difficulty, having lost my footing. I hadn't learnt to float and didn't know the first thing about swimming. Though I was only in the shallow end, but for the timely intervention of a plump lady who spotted my predicament, I could easily have drowned. When Mother found out I never went again.

Rosie was a slightly built girl with bright hazel eyes and brown bobbed hair curling around her ears (almost all of the girls wore their hair cut short), and a dimple would appear whenever she smiled. She always wore a gymslip of navy blue serge, a jumper with matching tie and long black stockings. I liked this school attire and, as soon as things looked up for our family — when Dad started on shift work — Mother bought me long black woollen gym stockings instead of the fawn-coloured cotton lisle ones which I hated; the elastic garters had never kept them up properly so they were forever wrinkling round my legs. I had to do without the gymslip, they were so much more expensive than home-made frocks. Our parents were never mean with us but they knew the value of money and saw no reason to fritter it away on blazers and gymslips. Most of our schoolmates dressed in a similar way to us with never anything resembling a uniform.

Our country school could never be classed as progressive, with its small asphalt playground for the boys and the hard earth one for the girls, but the people that I know who attended when I did recall those times with much nostalgia, harking back to certain episodes of their school days (probably not very funny at the time) with much amusement — so much for human nature. Easily forgotten are the occasions when a lady inspector called at the school to investigate the attendance of pupils and deal with truancy, scaring the culprit and everyone else as she approached in her black leathers, sitting astride her motorbike. (She was rather ahead of her time regarding fashion!)

Another one to cause an uneasy tremor to pass around the school was the nurse who examined our hair to make sure it was clean and free from 'vermin'. Most of us had little to be alarmed over, but it was her brusque way of dealing with us as we filed past that we didn't care for. If a child was unfortunate enough to have ring-worm, his or her hair would be cropped off and, if it was a girl, she would be sent to school wearing a mob-cap so that she looked presentable to others. The child would be made to sit apart from the rest of the class on the other side of the room. It must have been an awful feeling for a child to be segregated like that, but the rest of us took it for granted that this was how such things were dealt with.

With three or four classes sharing one room, there were bound to be distractions. It was impossible for children to be quiet all the time and, there being no privacy, we had to manage the best we could. By and large I think that we coped very well. As I recall these years, I see in my mind's eye a lad trying to tip-toe in his clogs across the bare boards as he left the room, doing his best to be silent.

Two or three girls would be chosen each year to attend cookery classes at Victoria Road Council School. This I found very enjoyable when my turn came. I also attended what is now the Northwich College of Art, every Monday afternoon, to take art lessons. Although we never ever painted pictures, we were taught to do lettering, basketwork, designs on white wood, lino cuts, etc. I was the only pupil at that time going from Rudheath School and I never cared for my solitary journey across the fields, down through Roker Park to Leftwich where the 'Technical School' as we called it was then situated, but, summer and winter, I stuck it out for almost three years.

I enjoyed a bit of responsibility when I was in the top

class. If the headmaster was extra busy correcting examination papers or dealing with school affairs he would ask me to read to the class to keep them quiet but, as we were a mixed school, it didn't take long for things to get out of hand if the teacher was absent for too long. The boys would soon start to tease but if they were caught 'acting the goat' they would be punished. Now and again when the stick was being used one or two of the big lads would rebel and there would be scuffling and bumping against the glass and wood partition. If you happened to be in the next room, you would all be aware of what was going on and the children would smirk and snigger, being safely on the other side.

One morning, my friend Rosie came to school and told me she was leaving to live near Manchester, where she had lived before. We exchanged keepsakes, small objects which we had in our pencil boxes, and before you could say 'Jack Robinson' she was gone. I never knew her address so we lost touch with one another — I wish it had been otherwise and that we could have met as the years went by.

I said earlier that my parents were now better off since Dad was on shift work and they were beginning to get on their feet. We felt the benefit in lots of ways — having a holiday was one. Our Mecca was New Brighton. We travelled by bus and train and when we reached Liverpool and boarded a tram with the magic words 'Pier Head' on the front I, for one, got the feeling that we had really arrived and were living life to the full. I still remember the feeling of excitement as we waited among the crowd on the pier for the ferry-boat — 'Royal Daffodil' — to draw alongside. The gang-plank was lowered and crowds of people surged forth, hurrying off to their destinations. As soon as we were allowed on board, we made our way to the top deck and found seats. Shortly, with a loud clanking of chains and a removing of gang-planks, the boat moved calmly away from the pier, leaving Liverpool behind. I didn't feel able to sit still but went and stood near the rails, fascinated to watch the white wake of the ferry-boat stretching out behind us further and further away. Later, I became blasé to our visits and took them in my stride.

As the ferry-boat gently nudged its way into New Brighton, on this first occasion, I could hardly wait to step onto the landing stage. We stayed for five days but when I later recounted our exploits to my classmates I said that we had gone for a week. Somehow, it seemed better to say a week, and anyway it was only two days short! I remember a man with only one leg who used to dive into the sea from the end of the pier — and a long drop it was, too. While he performed this feat, spectators would drop coins into his cap which lay on the sand.

Then there was the lighthouse where I stood to have my photo taken with Dad's box camera. When the film was developed, I was such a tiny figure that Mother couldn't resist pulling my leg about it, for I had insisted on standing by the lighthouse — which had taken very well! I remember the long stretch of golden sands where my sister made endless sandcastles and where we had our photo taken with Dad. I was wearing a kind of cloche hat made of straw, fashionable at the time, the brim of which was holding my head in a tight grip. We always seemed to be wearing our hats on every occasion.

As we walked along the promenade, we stopped to put our pennies in the slot machines that stood there — 'What the Butler Saw' type of thing. Then there was the Wax Works to be visited. This turned out to be 'musty fusty', a phrase my sister insisted on using. She was slightly afraid of the wax dolls in their dusty glass cases staring out at her and dressed in their dark red velvet clothes. I think her description of them was very apt. For the same reason, she was never partial to the Punch and Judy show which came to our school periodically. It was the dark red velvet again. Although we were to go to New Brighton on many occasions afterwards, I was never again to experience the thrill I had on my first visit.

In the Summer weather, Dad's work permitting, we would join forces on Saturday afternoons with Auntie Alice, Uncle Arthur and our cousin, walking three or four miles to a local beauty spot, Pickmere Lake. "No bottom to it, it's that deep", said some — a saying which always intrigued me. Setting off early after dinner, we used to take a short cut along the canal bank from our home to pick up our relations from Granny's, adding another two miles to our journey. I remember Dad and Uncle Arthur taking me for a ride in a rowing boat and, as I trailed my hand in the water, it was very, very cold. I felt a creepy feeling as I remembered the word 'bottomless'. There was a cottage by the lakeside where an old lady lived. She would charge two pence for a jug of boiling water to pour over our tea, which we had brought from home along with our milk and sugar. After playing and rambling in the meadows around the lake, we were always 'clemt to death', as Grandad would say when he was very hungry. The food brought for us soon disappeared as the fresh air aroused our appetites. These simple outings are recalled with great nostalgia by my mother and her sister, for it was a very happy period of their lives.

The 'Ice-Cream Man' of my schooldays travelled our avenues on foot, pushing along a brightly painted handcart with a well in the centre for the ice cream, kept cool by lumps of ice from an ice factory in town. The ice-cream man was known to one and all as 'Garibaldi'. This was not his real name but the name of the man for whom he had previously worked, who like himself was of Italian extraction. When his employer died, he took over the small business, but to the end of his days he was 'Garibaldi' to all of us.

One could not but admire this man's versatility, for during the winter months he travelled from Northwich, where he was based, to the villages around, selling chips. So, at a certain time of a winter's Saturday night, there would be the most unlikely looking 'chip shop' you ever saw, parked at the junction of the avenues. It was a cart, with a small cooking stove inside whose chimney poked up through the roof of the metal canopy. Much smoke issued forth as 'Mr Garibaldi' stoked up his fire in the iron stove. The whole contraption was set on two wheels and drawn along by a mule.

I remember the scene being lit up one dark cold night by the lamp which hung from its hook inside the cart. The animal stood patiently waiting, the cold wind blowing its long tail to and fro, while Garibaldi, with his black drooping moustache and wearing his old shabby coat, served a customer. He was a familiar figure for years. Later, when progress took over, a youth would ride around on a tricycle ringing a bell to attract customers and selling ice-cream wafers from a large box attached to the front of his machine — the first Walls ice-cream, as I remember.

The red-brick Working Men's Club, or Social Club, was known to us as 'The Empire Hall' and was built in the Twenties. Dad took us as children to see a play performed there one Saturday night, when a visiting repertory company used it as a theatre. The players had to walk from their dressing room at the front of the building, down the aisle through the audience to take their place on stage. This was how I was able to see my first actor in close-up, his face painted thickly with make-up. We also came here on Saturday afternoons, we children of the village, to the entertainment specially arranged for us, usually talent competitions and the like, which cost us twopence to get in. One of my friends would be accompanied by her two young sisters and brother — and it wasn't for the want of trying if they didn't all get in for twopence!

We had quite a variety of turns, from a ballet dancer — complete with pink tutu and satin slippers — or a girl dressed as an Irish colleen doing an Irish jig, to a girl dressed as a sailor dancing the Sailor's Hornpipe. There were usually more girls than boys willing to perform. We always ended the show with community singing, led by a favourite cartoon character of the day, 'Felix'. An actor would walk onto the stage dressed like a big black cat, in his furry outfit, and lead us in singing 'Felix kept on walking, kept on walking still, with his tail behind him, you would always find him', and so on. More favourites of the day were 'Bye-bye Blackbird', 'Home in Pasadena', and 'Horsey Keep Your Tail Up, Keep the Sun Out of My Eyes'. It was a very happy time as we let ourselves go and kept us out of mischief on a Saturday afternoon!

When Christmas Day came around it was a real family affair. The four of us always spent the day quietly at home, my sister and I content to play with our presents. There was no television, not even a radio until our neighbour's son, who was quite clever with such things, built us a crystal set. We would listen to 'Children's Hour', my sister and I sharing one set of headphones The run-up to Christmas was fun because of all the preparation for the holiday. Mother made her own Christmas puddings, one for us, one for Granny and one to be consumed in the New Year. When she was making them, the same ritual was always observed: they were never put on the fire to boil until we came home from school, so that we could stir the spicy mixture while making a wish at the same time. A silver sixpence was popped in for good luck.

We are so naive as children. I remember one Christmas morning in particular, when I was a little bit late for church. As I hurried as best I could down the lane, there was not another soul in sight; everywhere was white and silent, covered with snow. The only sound to be heard was made by my rubber wellingtons as I crunched along — they were a present from my parents, as was the small leather purse which dangled from my fingers on its chain. I felt very happy as I forged ahead leaving my footprints in the immaculate snow. All was well with the world.

Chapter Ten

J Parr's shop and the next door cottage had sunk to the level of their ground floor windowsills. (Photograph courtesy of Cheshire County Council Libraries and Archives)

Northwich has suffered greatly from subsidence over the years and I remember as a child seeing buildings leaning over at dangerous angles. Repair work went on constantly.

*M*other was in seventh heaven when Dad bought her a Singer sewing-machine. It was an attractive piece of furniture with a treadle and the whole machine could be put away neatly with a table top covering it. To protect its polished top, a white lace cloth was placed upon it when there was no sewing to be done and a plant was put in the middle to brighten it up. My sister and I were not allowed to touch this precious sewing-machine for a long while. I would try and get the gist of it through watching Mother, wait until she was otherwise engaged, then stealthily haul the machine from its hidden compartment. Spying my chance, I would imitate what I had seen my mother do, putting a bit of cloth under the needle, treadling with my feet and turning the small hand-wheel towards me at one and the same time. All was well until the wheel slipped backwards and the shuttle became locked with loose thread. When Mother came back into the house, there I would be, sitting miserably, unable to hide my wrong-doing and waiting for a good telling off, not to mention a clout.

It was always a challenge when I was left on my own and I just could not keep my hands off the sewing machine, always feeling sure that I could master its workings this time. But on one occasion I was really in for it, having got the shuttle once more tangled up with the cotton. Dad had to go into town to bring a mechanic from the Singer Sewing shop, as I had done something to its working that he couldn't put right. They had to pay for this service, of course, which quite upset me and I was much more grown-up and capable before I touched the sewing-machine again.

Dad had a mate at work whose wife ran a small business. From this source he bought a china tea-set and some fruit dishes, bringing them home one day for Mother. It was very nice china and I don't suppose he paid a lot for it but at the time of writing Mother is still in possession of most of it after all these years and I am sure that it would be quite expensive to buy today. One of the best things that was bought for us from my point of view was a 'cabinet' gramophone; this was a step forward from the old type with a horn. It was so named because that is what it looked like, with its small doors at the top to let out the sound and larger ones underneath in which to store the records. The top had a nice deep lid which closed over the machine. I believe it was a 'Cygnet' gramophone but I don't know which firm manufactured this type. It turned out to be a very good one lasting us for many years. The pleasure we got from this was boundless. Dad bought a parcel of records which though they were second hand were in very good condition and they included 'In a Monastery Garden', 'Bells across the Meadows' (Ketelby), 'Parted' composed by Tosti, one of Queen Victoria's favourite ballad writers (sung on our record by Count John McCormack), 'Whistler and his Dog', 'Poem' and lots of other semi-classical and good light music. Someone had good taste I must say and we could play these records for hours changing tiny steel needles as necessary, which were kept handy in a little tin box, and winding the gramophone handle in good time to stop the machine from running down and making a comical sound.

Another source of pleasure was the 'Magnet' comic which Mother bought for me every Friday. Sometimes she bought a bundle of back numbers of these magazines. I was in my element as she gave them to me. I would make my escape upstairs to lie on my bed and I was transported into another world as I avidly read through the adventures of Harry Wharton & Co. of Greyfriars School. I readily associated myself with the antics of this famous gang of schoolboys, being a bit of a tomboy myself. Although Bob Cherry with his fair curly hair was my hero, I could not help but feel sorry for Billy Bunter, the fat 'Owl of the Remove', who got himself into so many predicaments because of his greedy ways. I still remember the poem 'Ten Doughnuts', printed in one issue of the 'Magnet', a parody of some famous poem and the sad tale of Bunter's excessive passion for doughnuts, which was the death of him!

The adventures we got up to from time to time were of a different character altogether from the lads of posh Greyfriars School. There were limebeds nearby (and still are) where waste churned out from the chemical works has piled up over the years and been banked up until the sides are quite steep. We sometimes climbed to the top where iron bogies stood on the little railway track which encircled the perimeter of the limebeds. These were to be used the following day in disposal of waste, and around these we would play, sometimes trying to move the bogies along the track.

It was dangerous, to say the least, but we were eventually found out and the place soon ceased to be 'haunted' by us. I have never seen the tops of those limebeds since that time and, as the years have gone by, the name has changed — no longer 'limebeds' but 'lagoons' — and grass seed has been planted on the steep sides, the embankments now covered in a pleasant green. At first, men were sent to cut the grass with a machine until someone had a brainwave and sheep were used instead. Now the grass is always short and in Spring one can see lambs trotting after their mothers and hear them bleating.

There was a busy little family bakery owned by Mr and Mrs Batty, along Middlewich Road, where Mother used to buy her bread when we were children. The bakery (but not the shop) has long since gone, as has the picturesque old farmhouse that stood next door. This was a low red-brick building set well back from the road and I remember that it had a pear tree in the front garden. One of my classmates lived there and sometimes she would invite three or four of us to play in the large old barn across the yard from the house. It was no longer a working farm so we could play there to our heart's content. We would put on a show of sorts, pretending to be actors, dressing up in pieces of old curtains, old clothes or anything else we could find or lay our hands on — another outlet for our imagination.

As my sister and I became older, our parents started to take us to the pictures on a Saturday night. Most times we went to the old Central Cinema, which was burned down a number of years ago. As I remember, the place would be quite hazy with cigarette smoke and filled to capacity with people enjoying a night out at the end of a working week, and had quite a different atmosphere to that found today. There were few other diversions, and outings to the cinema were looked forward to with a great excitement.

We went to this same cinema on a Saturday afternoon, to

the matinées. The seats at the front were long bare wooden forms known locally as the 'bug rush' and you were charged a penny or twopence for the privilege of sitting there! How your neck would ache with the effort of looking up at the pictures on the huge screen. Just to one side, the lady pianist would be playing like mad to accompany the various scenes, partly obscured from us by a dark green curtain.

If you were feeling well off, you could pay a copper more and sit further away from the screen in a 'proper' seat. Very often the films would be of an adventurous nature, nearly always including a Red Indian saga. Of course, because they were silent films, we kept abreast of the action by reading the words which accompanied each picture as it flashed on to the screen. Saturday night's programme would be totally different, romantic dramas etc. with the big heart-throbs of the day, such as Ronald Coleman, Rudolph Valentino and Clive Brook; or comedies with famous stars like Charlie Chaplin, Harold Lloyd, Fatty Arbuckle and Buster Keaton.

Once in a while, we visited the Castle cinema at the other end of the town. There was an interval during the showing of films here, when two girls wearing black dresses, little fancy white aprons and caps would come around selling sweets and packets of pink nougat. Also, during the interval, the manager of the cinema, Mr Tom Sherlock, would walk onto the stage in his black suit, white shirt and bow tie, and entertain us by singing ballads. He had a good baritone voice and his performances were always very well received with much applause at the end.

Lastly, there was the Pavilion, an old black and white building which had seen better days. Originally a theatre, it later became a cinema, but during the Second World War it was used yet again as a theatre for variety acts. I saw one of the early American pop groups perform there, later to become famous as 'The Inkspots' with their hit song 'Whispering Grass', and Leslie Hutchinson, known all over the country as 'Hutch', accompanying himself on the piano. He sang romantic pop tunes of the day and, during his act, would produce a white hankie to dab the tears from his eyes.

Market day in Northwich was held on Fridays when I was a child, and I always enjoyed accompanying my mother to town if I got the chance. We often walked both there and back, struggling with the loaded shopping on our return. As we walked down Station Road, towards the main street, there were signs of the damage which salt-mining in the area had brought about. Passing the iron foundry we would come to a little sweet-shop that was below the level of the road and had two or three steps leading down into it. The window-sills of the cottages next door were almost level with the ground owing to subsidence. Shortly after this came Warrington Road, with the cottages on either side in similar condition. Grandad always spoke of Warrington Road as Mill Lane and the bridge at the bottom of the road as Mill Bridge, where lanes led to Marston, Marbury and Wincham. Near here there was once a pub known as the 'Witch and Devil', which disappeared sensationally through subsidence.

Walking on into Witton Street we would pass the Chinese laundry and then an open passage known as 'Pipe Makers Entry', where I believe there was once a small industry making clay pipes. A little further on there was a 'ginnel' which led into a cobbled courtyard with tiny cottages. Grandad's niece lived in one with her family.

A large, pleasant-faced woman, older than my mother, she was known to all of us as Aunt Mary Ellen. She used to call me 'Little Lenna' even when I was grown up. The cottage was kept spotlessly clean and I was quite taken with the kettle which hung on a chain over the fire. When it boiled she would swivel it back to the hob to make us a pot of tea. It was a really old cottage, as were the others in the cobbled courtyard, with water supplied from a stand-pipe in the yard.

As we progressed down town, we usually saw Uncle Charlie, Grandad's brother, propping up the General Post Office. He was broad and stout and getting on in years, and wearing his flat cap, red and white muffler and moleskin trousers. This was one of his favourite places, where he was content to stand and watch the world go by. He lived in Yorkshire Buildings (another cluster of little cottages with cobbled stone yards) and was a bachelor. At one time, he travelled the Northwich area selling his few wares of cottons, needles, thimbles and so on, but he had been a tradesman in his younger years, like his brothers. Before I left school, poor Uncle Charlie had died while sitting at his breakfast table. His accumulation of bits and pieces was left to Grandad to dispose of, including, I remember, a tricycle that he had been wont to use. A large, ungainly thing, seemingly with a mind of its own, it never went in the direction I wanted it to when I tried to ride it down the 'Backs' at Lostock.

People often enquire why Yorkshire Buildings were so called. I was once told that this was because men came down from Yorkshire with a pack-horse to sell their woollen cloth at Northwich market, staying overnight in the cottages before returning on their homeward journey. Whether this is a myth or really true I have no way of knowing, but it sounds feasible to me. At the bottom of Meadow Street, there had once been a cattle market and animals were regularly herded down Witton Street by farmers attending the auctions. Only the iron railings, used to enclose the cattle, remained when I was a child.

There was no Woolworth's or Marks and Spencer until I was almost at school-leaving age, and the hill on which they now stand was known as 'Ship Hill' — an old public house, The Ship Inn, had once stood there. The hill was steeper in those days, with stone sets on the road. Halfway down there was an entrance to a large timber yard and when a load of timber was being delivered the big cart-horses pulling the huge tree trunks on a trailer would be diverted from Witton Street in a semi-circle up Tabley Street and down Leicester Street to enable them to have a straight run across the main road and into the timber yard. They would never have been able to negotiate the sharp bend halfway down the hill otherwise. It was fascinating to me as a small child to watch the busy traffic being held up while the driver made a bee-line for the yard, the sparks flying from the horses' hooves as they pounded the stone sets with the heavy steel chains clanking against their sides. A large stone, polished with age and the weather, stood against the wall of Shields Pawnshop at the junction of

Leicester Street and Witton Street, supposedly to prevent the wheels of big heavy vehicles damaging the brick building as they passed. A similar stone stood against the wall of a pork butcher's shop at the entrance of Crum Hill.

As my mother and I wended our way to the market we would call in at the Maypole, where there was usually the sound of butter being busily patted into shape from the mound piled on the marble slab. I was always impressed with the speed and nimbleness of the grocer in his white coat and long white apron as he made up his packets of butter. Bergen's was another large grocer's shop, with the pleasant aroma of coffee to greet you as you walked through the door. Lipton's store, where Mother bought her Horniman's tea, was situated in the High Street, as was the Penny Bazaar' with its wide entrance where all sorts of haberdashery, small toys, etc. were displayed on the open counters.

A familiar figure to be seen on Market Day was Mr Makepeace, an apt name for a man of the Church, who preached at the Mission in Leicester Street. There you would see him in his black coat and cleric's hat setting up his small portable organ, a box placed conveniently for anyone wanting to make a contribution to his church. As I watched him sit down on a stool and begin to play, it always seemed to me that it was hard work as he leant forward, pressing rhythmically first with one foot and then the other on the wide pedals.

The old Market Hall was a large black and white building with a balcony running all the way around the second floor. A single row of stalls standing next to one another filled most of the space. After school, lads would run up and down the two flights of stairs irritating the stallholders and routing among the over-ripe fruit discarded by the green-grocers. Steps led up from the main part of the market hall to an area set aside for local farm produce — eggs, chickens, vegetables and flowers. An exit led out into Applemarket Street, where there stood an old lodging house, and big double doors made a side exit onto a cobbled stone yard hemmed in by old pubs.

Nearby there was an open-air market at Crum Hill, with its many assorted characters and all kinds of goods spread around the cobblestones. The man selling crockery would shout out his invitations to all and sundry, fanning the plates out like a conjurer. I was sure that he would drop them but he never did! The man selling chocolates and sweets would place one box of goodies on the top of another until, balancing them all, he would cry "Who'll give me two shillings for this little lot?" If there was no immediate reply, another bar of chocolate would be added and, as a last resort, a chocolate walnut whip would be slapped on top of everything else. We certainly got value for our money in those days. Once, a man selling blankets, towels, and all sorts of household goods, annoyed at the poor response of his onlookers, throw a very large linen tablecloth on the damp cobblestones and offered it for almost nothing. I remember it was a lovely cloth.

It was like a variety act sometimes where two men served at the same stall. One would be very quiet while the other was quite a comic, drawing the crowds close around him and putting people in a good humour. At one period of time, Mother says, a fellow would bring his van to Crum Hill loaded with parcels, a mystery to everybody. It appeared that he bought these parcels all sealed up from a pawnbroker in the town — 'unredeemed goods' — and would offer them for sale to the public for, say, two shillings or something similar. You had no idea what you would be buying so took your chance when you handed over your money, though Mother says that she never took a chance and never found out what any of these parcels contained! When it became dark early in the winter months, stalls would be lit up by naphtha flares which hissed and blew about in the wind, only partly protected from the elements.

On our way home we often called in at the herbalist's shop in the main street, known to everybody as 'Pop Hornby's', where, on a cold day, it was comforting to buy a hot blackcurrant drink. There would always be a good selection of cordials to choose from out of the tall urns that sat on the high counter, gently simmering away – including Oxo, raspberry, peppermint, sarsaparilla, ginger beer. It was a favourite haunt for the lads on a Saturday afternoon and, as the shop was only small, it was soon full. There were wooden forms to sit upon as you sipped your cordial at the iron tables, no frills or anything fancy, just the basics, but it was patronised by many people.

Around the walls hung a set of black and white Victorian prints, entitled 'When the Bottle Came to the House'. My mother said that it put years on her to look at them! No matter how many times we called in at the shop, I could never resist taking another look. In a way the sketches were not unlike 'The Rake's Progress' by William Hogarth, illustrating a man's dissipation and downfall. In this case, his downfall came when be brought alcohol into his happy home, causing him to neglect his wife and children. The last sketch showed him shivering in the corner of a prison cell, awaiting trial for the murder of his wife in a drunken brawl. The moral was very clear. Melodramatic as the sketches were, I should think that they would be quite valuable nowadays, and I am sure that many people in Northwich will remember them.

Northwich has suffered greatly from subsidence over the years and I remember as a child seeing buildings leaning over at dangerous angles and a large bank in the Bull Ring which had to be hoisted up on timbers. Repair work went on constantly. Mother attended a small school in Leicester Street, known to everybody as 'Dickie King's School'. The building at that time was subsiding and was held up by baulks or large timbers. Round about on the ground lay pieces of rock salt, which the small infants would pick up and lick. As the subsidence rapidly became worse, staff and children were moved wholesale into the Methodist Chapel in the main street, until the Council school being built in Victoria Road was completed.

Since that time, Northwich has turned into a most pleasant market-town, with an attractive shopping precinct around the area where Crum Hill once stood. Not far from the Bull Ring, where hundreds of people used to gather to listen to the Salvation Army Band on New Year's Eve, is one of the town's two swing bridges over the River Weaver. The bell still rings out shrilly now and again to warn the busy traffic of an approaching vessel, these days mostly yachts with their high masts.

When I was a child, I would be drawn by the warning bell, for I loved to stand among the crowd as they waited impatiently to cross the river. It gave me a small thrill to watch the bridge turn slowly allowing a large, heavily laden boat to pass by. This used to be a regular occurrence in the life of the town, but it happens very seldom nowadays.

The greater part of my last year at school was spent being taught 'Housewifery', along with several other girls from schools in the Northwich area, at a house in Orchard Street, close to Victoria Road Council School. Usually two girls were sent from each school to attend every day. I couldn't begin to recount the capers we got up to whilst trying to master the art of housekeeping. Miss Beetson was a tall, plump lady with a Scottish accent, rather strict and serious, and was employed by the Education Authorities to instruct us in the correct way to run a household and to instil in us a sense of responsibility. Her patience must have been sorely tried as she dealt with one class after another of adolescent schoolgirls.

I remember the look of horror on her face one day when a member of our class badly scorched her best night-dress while ironing it. "My nun's veiling night-dress!" she gasped, at least twice. The material was specially delicate and fine, and the poor girl doing the ironing looked as though she had committed a criminal offence. The rest of us made our-selves scarce, getting on with other chores, but still feeling sympathetic towards our classmate. Shortly afterwards, another girl dropped a bowl containing lentils on the floor and thousands of them were scattered everywhere. She was asked to fetch the 'long switch'. Not being used to some of Miss Beetson's sayings, neither the girl nor the rest of us knew what she meant, and as the teacher was irritable enough already, nobody had the courage to ask.

Someone said that it was the vacuum cleaner at the top of the stairs, so two of us went to fetch it, in the mistaken belief that this was the object required. I remember that it looked as though it had come out of the ark, it was so heavy and cumbersome. When the teacher's eyes alighted on it, she became even more angry, and we were chased back up the stairs with it, almost collapsing with laughter, for all that she had meant the girl to bring in the first place had been an ordinary sweeping brush!

The day came when I was fourteen and ready to leave school. Little did I realise that this would coincide with another event in our small family which would turn our way of life topsy-turvy — Dad lost his job. It was 'goodbye' to any plans that my parents had had for me. We survived, though, due to my mother's and father's strength of character and I can now look back on those difficult times with great appreciation for all their hard work.

Lenna and Jim pictured shortly before their marriage

'WE'LL GATHER LILACS...'

When **Lenna Bickerton's** book "Memories of a Cheshire Childhood" was published in 1996, her life changed. The book became the Léonie Press's best selling local title and wherever she went, Lenna would meet readers who thanked her for describing so vividly a world which has vanished for ever.

Though devastated by widowhood, Lenna – now in her eighties – decided to write another book covering her life during the Depression and the early War years. A lover of music, literature and art, the bright and intelligent girl was unable to go to college for financial reasons. Instead she worked in a biscuit factory, briefly as a maid, behind the counter at Woolworths and in her parents' greengrocer's shop. When she was 14 she met her future husband, Jim, who spent years trying to get a job after being laid off by ICI. During their long courtship and after they were married, their pleasures were simple – walking, cycling, gathering lilac and wild flowers, appreciating the countryside and enjoying one another's company. This book is a hymn to their enduring love affair as well as a fascinating description of Cheshire in the 'thirties and 'forties.

Lenna died in November 1999 when she was writing the last chapter. The book was completed by her daughter, **June Hall** and launched on March 7, 2001 at the College of Art in Northwich alongside an exhibition of Lenna's paintings.

"We'll Gather Lilacs..." (ISBN 978-1-901253-21-4) is available through bookshops or from Léonie Press, 13 Vale Road, Hartford, Northwich, Cheshire CW8 1PL, price £5.99 (please add £1 for postage and packing if ordering from publisher).

Léonie Press specialises in local history and autobiography

MID-CHESHIRE MEMORIES: Volume One
E E Osborne, Geoffrey Mellor, Peter Buckley, Bruce Fisher
(ISBN 978-1-901253-28-3)

The first book in a series on ways of life and occupations in Mid-Cheshire that have now changed out of all recognition or vanished for ever. The three male authors tell of their childhoods and teenage years, while Nellie Osborne writes about her agricultural worker father's life at work and at home. Featuring: The Horseman and his Family; The Apprentice Mechanic's Tale; The Apprentice Fitter's Tale, and The Fireman's Tale of the End of Steam. Maps and photographs included. **£8.99**

A HISTORY OF WHISTON – *From the Stone Age to the Plastic Age*
William K Blinkhorn (ISBN 978-1-901253-38-2)

William K Blinkhorn's wide-ranging book is a fascinating and readable dip into the past of the Merseyside coal-mining town of Whiston. He traces the story of Whiston from its Stone Age beginnings to the closure of one of its most modern industries, a plastics factory. He looks at numerous facets of the town's history including the lords of the manor, place-name derivations, religion, schools, agriculture and industry. **£8.99**

A HOUSE WITH SPIRIT
A Dedication to Marbury Hall
Jackie Hamlett and Christine Hamlett (ISBN 978-1-901253-19-1)

The authors spent three years researching the history of Marbury Hall near Northwich and tracing the lives of its aristocratic and often high-spirited owners. As clairvoyants they have their own theories about its famous ghosts, the Marbury Lady and the Marbury Dunne. They have tapped into the memories they believe still hang around the site of the demolished hall which have enabled them to communicate with its essence. **£8.99**

WOOLLYBACK
Alan Fleet (ISBN 978-1-901253-18-4)

This moving and evocative novel is set in Winsford, Cheshire. The author studies the prejudice between the inhabitants of Over and Wharton in one generation and between the Liverpudlian overspill 'Scousers' and the native 'Woollybacks' in the next, through the eyes of a father and son – who are united by love and divided by mutual misunderstanding. **£8.99**

A NUN'S GRAVE
A novel set in the Vale Royal of England
Alan K Leicester (ISBN 978-1-901253-08-5)

The Nun's Grave at Vale Royal Abbey has been a source of mystery and ghostly stories for generations of Mid-Cheshire folk. Alan K Leicester's frightening experience there as a young man led him to undertake years of research into the subject and he has woven his findings into a thought-provoking novel on two time-scales. The 14C fates of novice nun Ida Godman and young monk John of Dutton become inextricably entwined with the present-day lives of newly-weds Ian and Jane who buy a house on the site of the abbey. The author stresses that his enthralling book is fiction and not scholarship.

£7.99

DIESEL TAFF
From 'The Barracks' to Tripoli
Austin Hughes (ISBN 978-1-901253-14-6)

Austin Hughes was born in February 1922 at 'The Barracks', a group of flea-ridden cottages deep in rural North Wales. His book tells how he grew up as an abstemious god-fearing country lad, innocent of the world outside. From childhood he had loved heavy machinery and he learned to drive trucks and bulldozers. Then in 1940 he was called up to join the Royal Engineers. This was to be an experience which changed the young Welshman's life and earned him his nick-name 'Diesel Taff'. By the end of the war, he'd been to 18 countries, travelling thousands of miles across deserts and mountains, transporting heavy plant, building roads and air strips, clearing avalanches and ferrying refugees. The book gives fascinating insights into life in pre-war rural Wales as well as describing the daily experiences and duties of an R.E. sapper driver in WW2. **£8.99**

THE WAY WE WERE
Omnibus edition incorporating Over My Shoulder and Another's War
Les Cooper (ISBN 978-1-901253-07-8)

This book is an omnibus edition of Les Cooper's Crewe memories "Over My Shoulder" and "Another's War", originally published separately in 1996 by Crewe and Nantwich Borough Council when the author was mayor, and now reprinted by popular demand.

The first work describes his childhood in the railway town during the Depression and the second his war experiences as an apprentice in a reserved occupation at the LMS Railway Works. **£7.99**

**All these books can be ordered from Léonie Press,
13 Vale Road, Hartford, Northwich, Cheshire CW8 1PL
Tel 01606 75660 Fax: 01606 77609 e-mail: anne@leoniepress.com
For the latest information visit our website: www.leoniepress.com**